Mussolini and Italy

C.C. Bayne-Jardine, M.A., M. Ed.
Headmaster, Henbury School, Bristol

LONGMAN

LONGMAN GROUP UK LIMITED
Longman House
Burnt Mill, Harlow, Essex CM20 2JE, England
and Associated Companies throughout the World.

First published 1966
Fifteenth impression 1987

Produced by Longman Group (FE) Ltd
Printed in Hong Kong

ISBN 0-582-20426-7

Acknowledgements

We are grateful to the following for permission to reproduce
copyright material:
Cassell & Co. Ltd and Houghton Mifflin Company for an extract
from *Second World War*, Vol. II by Sir Winston S. Churchill;
Macdonald & Co. (Publishers) Ltd and Coward McCann Inc. for an
extract from *Pagine di Critica Fascista: Vent'anni e un giorno* which is
quoted as translated in *The Day of the Lion* by Roy MacGregor-Hastie
(Macdonald 1963); the Ministry of Defence for the Italian Army
Song from 'The Trouble with Italians' published in *Army Bureau
Current Affairs Pamphlet* No. 35, 1942; Odhams Books Ltd for extracts
from *Mussolini—Study of a Demagogue* by Sir Ivone Kirkpatrick; the
author and Jonathan Cape Ltd for an extract from *Fontamara* by
Ignazio Silone (translated by David & Mosbacher), and the South
African Government Printer, Pretoria, for an extract from. Major
Mors: 'Skorzeny Bubble', published in *Kommando*, Vol. 4, No. 32–33.

For permission to reproduce photographs we are grateful to the
following:
Barnaby's Picture Library—page 116; Camera Press—page 72;
Imperial War Museum—pages 1, 5, 93, 98, 100, 104 and 105;
Keystone Press—pages 21, 36, 65 and 114; London Express News
and Feature Services—pages 39, 42 (except violinist), 49 bottom, 70
and 106; Paul Popper—pages 2, 9, 13, 18, 23, 41, 50, 52 and 53;
Pictorial Press—page 48; *Punch*—pages 57, 59 and 92; Radio Times
Hulton Picture Library—pages 4, 29, 42 (violinist) and 45;
Syndication International—pages 44 and 46; Ullstein Bilderdienst—
pages 31, 49 top, 56, 66, 68, 78, 89, 101 and 109; United Press
International (UK) Ltd.—page 60.

Preface

Mussolini ruled Italy for twenty-three years. He aroused feelings of hatred and of love, of contempt and of admiration. To many he still remains a fascinating riddle. His life was full of incident and I have tried to tell his story and then leave it to you to draw your own conclusions about Mussolini.

I make no claim to original work on this subject. My debt to Sir Ivone Kirkpatrick, Denis Mack Smith and F. W. Deakin, will be obvious. Perhaps I should draw attention to Sir Ivone Kirkpatrick's tentative judgment on Mussolini. He states that he is inclined to agree with Grandi who summed up his feelings with the two words: 'Poor Mussolini.' I hope that you will soon be able to discover whether or not you agree with this verdict.

Finally I should like to thank all those who have helped and encouraged me. I trust that they and others may enjoy trying to solve the riddle posed by Mussolini and his Italy.

C. C. BAYNE-JARDINE

Contents

Outline of Events

1911–1912 Libyan War

1914   First World War began

1919   Treaty of Versailles

1925   Locarno Pact

1933   Hitler, German Chancellor

1934   Murder of Austrian Chancellor, Dollfuss

1936   Spanish Civil War

1938   March. Germany annexed Austria. Sept. Munich crisis

1939   Poland invaded by Germany

1940   Axis pact

1945   7 May. Surrender of Nazi Germany

          2 Sept. Unconditional surrender by Japan

          24 Oct. Official beginning of the United Nations

1957   Treaty of Rome. Common Market set up

1 The Riddle of Mussolini

Mussolini wearing Fascist uniform, 1938

> '*He is a rabbit: a phenomenal rabbit: he roars. People who see him and who do not know him mistake him for a lion.*'
>
> Serrati of Mussolini, 1919

A brief glance at the outline of events during Mussolini's life shows that for more than twenty years Mussolini controlled the destiny of the Italian people. He reached the summit of his popularity on the evening of 9 May 1936 when, from the balcony of the Palazzo Venezia in Rome, he announced the creation of a new empire. The Emperor of Ethiopia had fled in a British battleship and the Italian Marshal Badoglio had occupied Addis Ababa. Ethiopia is the ancient name for the area of north-eastern Africa bordering on the Red Sea which is now called Abyssinia. The Italian people awaited their Duce's announcement with mounting excitement. As well as those who crushed beneath the floodlit balcony in Rome, there were others who crouched over radio sets and who clustered round loudspeakers set up all over Italy.

At half past ten trumpets blared and a twenty-one-gun

The crowd 'crushed beneath the floodlit balcony in Rome', May 1936

salute boomed out. At thirty-three minutes after ten Mussolini strode onto his balcony. His face was strangely pale under the floodlights and it stood out starkly against the grey and black uniform of the Fascist militia which he was wearing for the occasion. He stood for some minutes, his legs splayed and his jaw out-thrust, savouring the cheering. He was like a rock against which the waves of cheering thundered. Then his hand swept up to switch off the adulation and he began to speak in his clear, sonorous voice:

'Officers, non-commissioned officers and men of all the armed forces in Italy and East Africa; Blackshirts of the Revolution, Italian men and women at home and throughout the world, hearken:

'A great event has been accomplished. The destiny of Abyssinia has been sealed today, in the Fourteenth Year of the Fascist Era.

'Every knot has been cut by our shining sword, and the African victory remains in the history of our country, complete and pure like the legionaries who have fallen.

'Italy has at last her Empire—a Fascist Empire. For fourteen years she has looked forward to it. . . .'

Mussolini went on to say that the King of Italy would take the title of Emperor of Abyssinia and that the great era of an Italian empire, an empire of peace, had begun. He ended with the words: 'Raise up your banners, stretch forth your arms, lift up your hearts and sing to the Empire which appears in being after fifteen centuries on the fateful hills of Rome.

'Will you be worthy of this Empire?'

'Si, si, si,' shouted the crowd. Cheering and the swelling chant of 'Duce! Duce! Duce!' drowned the last few words of his speech. Mussolini remained impassive and perhaps it is understandable that some should feel that, like the Roman conquerors of old, he had become a god.

Six months later enthusiasm had dwindled. The business of empire-building lost its charm as it became more and more expensive and some of the hollowness of this new Roman empire became apparent. Still Mussolini had shown that, as he himself said, 'The crowd loves strong men. The crowd is like a woman. . . . Everything turns upon one's ability to control it like an artist.'

3

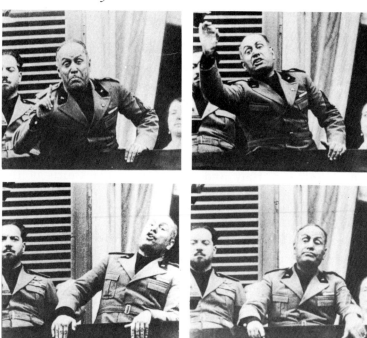

Mussolini controls the crowd 'like an artist'

How did Mussolini do this? How did the son of a black-smith succeed in controlling the Italian nation? How did a man, who had been in prison on eleven occasions, who had been in turn a school-teacher, a Socialist agitator, a journalist and a model corporal during the 1914–18 War, strut upon the European stage? Was he a rabbit who, by his own brilliant propaganda, deceived the world that he was a lion?

2 Italy in 1919

'Had we returned home in 1916, out of the suffering and the strength of our experiences we might have unleashed a storm. Now if we go back we will be weary, broken, burnt out, rootless, and without hope. We will not be able to find our way any more.
And men will not understand us . . .'
(All Quiet on the Western Front, E. M. Remarque)

The Italians in 1919 had no doubt that the rest of the world did not understand them. The feeling of disillusion after the 1914–18 War was very strong in Italy. This feeling was carefully fostered in the years after the war but the Italians felt humiliated by the memory of Caporetto when 700,000 men had retreated for 100 miles in panic. Italian soldiers felt that their allies had forgotten that at least 460,000 Italians had been killed in the effort of defeating Germany and Austria-Hungary and that in October 1918 the Italian army smashed the Austrians at Vittorio Veneto.

As it was soldiers returned home uncertain of what they had

Italian soldiers in the snow on Monte Nero near Caporetto

been fighting for, and not very proud of the way in which they had fought. Before questions could be asked about the regiments that broke and ran at Caporetto the Italians began to brag about the land that had been won for Italy. All over Italy men opened the litres of wine for the toast to victory. As the evenings grew cooler so the arguments in the cafés grew warmer and as time went on tinged with bitterness. Why had Italy entered the conflict in 1915? The simple answer was that she wanted land. The returned soldiers and the café politicians all agreed that this was so.

On 26 April 1915 Britain, France, Russia and Italy had signed the secret Treaty of London. Italy had been promised the area shaded on the map and possibly part of Turkey and some of the German territories in Africa. Now the Italians expected their full share for their part in the war and because they were not proud of that part in the war they urged their demands. The United States had not signed the Treaty of London and President Wilson stood firmly by his own fourteen points with regard to Italy. Of these points Article 9 laid down that the Italian frontiers should be 'readjusted along clearly recognizable lines of nationality'. Over these 'lines of nationality' argument raged. The Italian veterans from the battlefields pointed out that they deserved Dalmatia and, of course, Fiume. The café politicians agreed and many grimy fingers were dipped in red wine to sketch out the frontier between Italy and Yugoslavia on marble-topped tables all over the country.

Round the highly polished table at the peace conference there was little interest in the problem of the Italian frontiers. Orlando who represented Italy at the Versailles peace conference found his position difficult. The Allies did not bother to hide the fact that they had little time for Italian problems. Italy had been useful as a balance against Austria-Hungary. In 1918 Austria-Hungary had been destroyed. Orlando himself felt that the Treaty of London had been made against a foe who no longer existed. Wilson was tactless and did not bother to soothe ruffled nationalist feelings. Wilson even appealed to the Italian people over the heads of their government. As a protest in April 1919 Orlando withdrew from Paris for two weeks.

Italian gains, 1919

In fact Italy did receive most of the promised lands of 1915. Under the Treaty of St Germain with Austria she received the Trentino, South Tyrol, Trieste and Istria. Her north-eastern frontier was safe, but the eastern frontier sketched out so busily by Italians was more complex. Italians lived in many of the

7

cities while the countryside was predominantly Slav. The interest centred on the city of Fiume. The Italians regarded this city as part of their reward, and an important part as it was connected by rail to Vienna and Budapest. Fiume might rival Trieste as an outlet on the Adriatic, so the Italian demands grew stronger. D'Annunzio spoke for many of his countrymen when he claimed: 'Dalmatia belongs to Italy by divine right as well as human law.'

The squabbles over the eastern frontier were to drag on after 1919. There was no easy solution but the Italian people felt that they were being cheated by foreign politicians who had little interest in the Italian frontier. In addition they began to feel that their own politicians had not done all they could for the true interests of Italy.

The returned soldiers felt increasing bitterness when they turned from boasting about battle and from the victory celebrations to the task of finding a job. War had brought home to the world the fact that Italy was not a great power. Now the humiliated Italians were beginning to count the cost. The Treasury announced in 1930 that the cost of the war had been 148 billion lire. This fantastic sum was twice as much as all government expenditure between 1861 and 1913. Furthermore allied economic help ceased at the end of the war and the Italian economy went to pieces. The soldiers could not find a job and many who had stayed at home were unemployed. Some soldiers took up their rifles again and left home to join one of the groups of deserters who prowled in brigand bands over parts of Italy. The majority returned to the cafés where they had celebrated victory and sat around with nothing to do and no money for wine.

Soon they began to blame the government for allowing such things to happen. The government was an easy target. As early as 1861 Mazzini, an Italian republican, had written bitterly, 'I thought to call up the soul of Italy and I see only its corpse'. The unemployed and frustrated Italian in 1919 endorsed Mazzini's view. After all they had fought and worked for their country and deserved something better than unemployment and starvation.

Unfortunately the Italian government had no tradition of firm and enlightened leadership. The new Kingdom of Italy in 1861 had faced various problems and these problems still existed in 1919. It was only too easy for the disillusioned soldiers and their friends to criticize their government.

The problem of poverty and the division between North and South was still unsolved in 1919. To the bored and hungry men of 1919 any meal would have seemed a feast but many Italians already suffered from diseases brought on by their starchy diet. In the years 1881–84 a team of doctors inspected 3,672 Sicilian sulphur miners to discover how many were fit for military service. They passed 203 as being fit. Malaria, cholera and other diseases were rife. In 1898 there had been bread riots (the *Fatti di Maggio*) in various parts of the country.

A market scene in Rome. 'Italy was a poor country . . .'

Italy was a poor country and the strain of the war was too much for her weak economy. Before the 1914–18 War it was possible to make ends meet by exporting wine, olives, fruit, leatherwork, woodwork and glass to pay for coal, iron, petrol and cotton. Any debit balance was made up by tourists spending foreign currency in Italy and the money sent home by emigrant Italians. In 1919 there were few demands for luxury Italian goods and there were even fewer tourists. Distrust between the more industrial North and the primitive South with its secret societies and its brigands was deepened by the growing disillusion and poverty. No wonder that many gathered in groups in cafés and on the street corners could be heard to say: 'In the next war we had better be defeated, if this is what it means to be one of the victorious powers.'

The Roman Catholic Church, to which nearly all Italians belonged, was little help at this time. Candles were lit and placed before statues of favourite saints in churches all over Italy. The wax melted and the candle flames grew longer and then expired. With them expired the hope that the Roman Catholic Church could do anything practical for the majority of Italians. When Italy became a united kingdom with Rome as its capital the Pope lost his lands and chose to pose as 'the prisoner of the Vatican'. In the early stages of the new Italian kingdom Roman Catholics were not supposed to take part in political life. This ban remained into the twentieth century though many of the faithful disobeyed it, and 60 per cent of the nation did vote. In 1903 Pius X, 'the Pope of the poor and humble', gave permission to Catholics to take part in politics to maintain the safety of the social order. In 1919 the Church was still reluctant to come to terms with the State and the candles burnt in thanks for victory did not bring any practical change.

The growing discontent in Italy had little impact on the politicians. Politics had become a great game of chance. Politicians did not bother about the people; they kept themselves in power by a system called 'transformism'. This was a system by which a leader gathered support from every possible source and so avoided topics which might split groups. The political leader, Crispi, when out of office in 1886 described this system of influence: 'There is pandemonium in parliament when an important vote comes along, as government agents run through rooms and down corridors collecting votes and promising subsidies, decorations, canals and bridges.' Elections were a farce as only a small percentage of the population had the vote even after Giolitti had widened the franchise in 1912. Many of the voters could neither read nor write and symbols had to be used on ballot papers. The government encouraged local officials to use their influence to make certain the government candidate was elected. Names of opposition voters were often erased from election lists and criminals were released from prison in return for votes. The only check on a minister was that his supporting groups might break up. 'A gust of wind, and these leaves which call themselves deputies will be blown about and mixed up anew.' In a parliament where the Speaker was often showered with paper darts and where fights sometimes broke out such 'gusts of wind' were common enough. In the seventy-five years before 1922 there were sixty-seven ministries, nearly a ministry every year. Little wonder that the Italians expected little real action from their government in 1919.

The disillusion of the hungry and bored groups all over Italy was made deeper by the fact that they had expected so much after the war. In the past their attention had often been diverted from internal problems in Italy by glittering promises of a great colonial empire. Governments were able to pretend that Italy was a great power because other powers in Europe used her as a balance against Austria-Hungary. Bismarck with his usual realism pointed out that Italy had a big appetite but very poor teeth.

The Italians had always been encouraged by their political leaders to think in terms of a Mediterranean Empire. As early as 1881–82 the Italian government had made efforts to gain colonies in Tunisia and Egypt. In face of opposition from France and Britain they had turned their attention to the Red Sea where the Italian colony of Eritrea had been set up in 1890 (map on page 61). This attempt to control an area in Africa was halted sharply when four badly organized columns of Italian troops were defeated by the Ethiopian tribesmen at Adowa in 1896. This humiliation led to the political defeat of the prime minister, Crispi, and to a temporary halt to colonial expansion. The propaganda value of colonial enterprises was too great to be neglected by Italian politicians for long. In spite of the defeat at Adowa a protectorate was set up over much of Somaliland. A military expedition was even sent to

China in 1899. This expedition was an expensive failure and, as a result, the Italians turned back to Africa. By 1905 an Italian bank, the Banco di Roma, was the largest landowner in Libya and controlled much of the sponge industry there. The bank encouraged the government to think in terms of military conquest and in September 1911 war was declared on Turkey, the overlord of Libya. The military expedition was ill prepared and the commander, General Caneva, hugged the coast where he was protected by the naval guns of the Italian fleet. During this campaign planes were used for bombing raids for the first time in history. The Italian pilots were unable to find many targets in the desert and most of the bombs exploded harmlessly in the sand. The war dragged on and spread to the Dodecanese islands between Crete and Turkey. The Italians took Rhodes in 1912. The European powers were concentrating on the rising power of Germany and on the changes in the Balkans which sprang from Turkish weakness. As a result the Italians were able to make their own terms with Turkey. Italy gained Libya and the Dodecanese Islands and in return paid a large sum towards the Turkish national debt. Italy had won some colonies at great cost and, although there were many in Italy who doubted the value of such colonies, the public were encouraged to believe in the glamour of empire-building.

The Italians were used to their leaders claiming that Italy was a first-class power. They could not face the fact that they were not one and could not be one on their resources.

Italy desperately needed a leader to bring her through the postwar depression. The government was faced by the problems of poverty, political inexperience and national disillusionment. The people had been encouraged to expect greatness and in 1919 they were hungry and humiliated. They looked hopefully for a strong leader.

3   Mussolini

'One day I shall astonish the world.'

Mussolini to his mother.

Childhood 1883–1901

On 29 July 1883 a thunderbolt struck and smashed the top of
the statue of the imperial eagle in Vienna. At two in the afternoon of the same day Mussolini was born in Varano di Costa

Mussolini's birthplace

in Romagna. His father was a blacksmith with fiery socialist
views and named his first-born Benito Amilcare Andrea, after
the Mexican revolutionary, Benito Juarez, and two other
Italian revolutionaries. His mother was a school-teacher who
was gentle and deeply religious. Later Mussolini was to write:
'To displease her was my one fear.'

He had few fears in these early years. Sometimes he worked

13

the bellows for his father and would receive a sharp blow if he allowed his attention to wander but for most of the time he roamed wild. He would return home scratched and triumphant from a poaching expedition or a fight with stones with other boys. Then he would swallow the simple meal of vegetable soup and cakes made out of flour and water before wandering off again to quarrel with other children or to sit dreaming of the future.

At the age of nine Mussolini was sent away to school at Faenza. His parents hoped that the monks who ran the school would tame their wild son. Mussolini was really miserable when his father lifted him out of the donkey cart and left him with the stern monks. He hated the restrictions of school life and found that the smell of incense made him feel sick. He particularly resented the fact that boys were served different food according to the fees they paid and that the lowest grade were served bread crawling with ants. One of his only friends was a boy who used to allow Mussolini to bang him on the head with a brick to show how thick his skull was. Violence often flared up and one day Mussolini hurled an inkwell at one of the monks. Then he quarrelled with an older boy and stabbed him with a penknife. The headmaster wished to expel him but in the end he was allowed to stay until the end of the term.

Mussolini's parents then decided to send Benito to a school for the sons of elementary school-teachers at Forlimpopolo. Here Mussolini was happier because for the first few years he boarded out in the town. He worked well and was renowned for his powerful speeches to his fellows and his flowing black tie. He managed to organize a successful demonstration against the standard of bread served and was later chosen by the masters to make a public speech in honour of the composer Verdi. It was typical of Mussolini that he should take the opportunity to make a socialist speech, which was briefly mentioned in the socialist paper *Avanti*.

During his last years at school Mussolini was noted for his interest in politics and his rebellious behaviour. He checked his wilder impulses and in July 1901 he gained the diploma of an elementary teacher. He received the highest mark in the examination in history, literature and singing. He could now begin to 'astonish the world'.

Youth 1901–12

At first Mussolini failed to find outlet for the talents which he felt the world should recognize. He failed to get the first two jobs for which he applied and eventually he became an elementary school-teacher. Within less than a year he moved on to seek his fortune in Switzerland. He was probably encouraged to emigrate by the fact that he was due to do his military service and by the quarrel that he had with the local mayor. In any case he did not find his early days in Switzerland easy. He worked carrying bricks until his muscles ached and his cheap shoes wore out. Much of the time he was out of work and in a letter to a friend he described one of his days in Switzerland.

'From ten until eleven I stay in the public lavatory, from eleven to twelve under an old barge. The wind blows from Savoy and is cold. I return into the town and spend the rest of the night under the Grand Pont. In the morning I look at myself out of curiosity in the windows of a shop. I am unrecognizable. I meet a man from Romagna. I tell him briefly of my affairs. He laughs at me. I curse him. He puts his hand in his pocket and gives me fifty centesimi. I thank him. I hasten to the shop of a baker and buy a piece of bread. I continue walking towards the wood. I feel as though I had a fortune. Having got a long way from the centre of the city I bite into my bread with the ferocity of a Cerberus. For twenty-six hours I had not eaten.'

During his vagrant life Mussolini had many affairs with women. His thinking at this time was much influenced by Angelica Balabanoff, a Communist from the Ukraine, who was working amongst the Italian Socialists in Switzerland. Under her guidance Mussolini attended lectures and dipped into the writings of such philosophers as Nietzsche and Hegel as well as the works of Marx. For a time he was even attracted by Buddhism.

Mussolini was expelled from Switzerland on account of his violent political opinions and he went to France where he taught for a time. From there he wandered to Zurich and Berne. During this period he won the reputation of being a wild young Socialist who encouraged strike action and who had once fought a pistol duel in defence of his views. In 1904 the birth of an heir to the Italian King led to the declaration of a free pardon for all deserters. Mussolini decided to return to Italy and do his military service. This he did with the 10th Bersaglieri Regiment at Verona. His military service was uneventful, but during that period his mother died. Her death upset Mussolini greatly and marked the end of any real family ties for him.

After his discharge in 1906 Mussolini returned to his wanderings. He taught for a time, made love to many women, wrote articles for Socialist newspapers, and engaged in local politics. In 1908 he was sent to prison for disturbing the peace and on his release he was offered a job in Austria as secretary of a local branch of the Socialist party and editor of their weekly newspaper. Mussolini thoroughly enjoyed this work though he thought the Socialists of the Trentino lacked spirit. He himself was aggressive and attacked established institutions, especially the Church, with gusto. As a result he was deported from Austria to Italy where he became secretary to the Socialists at Forli. Once again he used his position to put forward violent views. At this time he went to live with Rachele Guidi who became his wife though there was no official state ceremony until 1915. Rachele followed Mussolini throughout his life and made him a quiet and good wife in spite of his flagrant infidelity.

In 1911 Mussolini made speeches and wrote articles urging a general strike in Forli. When order had been restored by troops he was arrested and sent to prison. His trial made him a local Socialist hero and he emerged at the party conference at Reggio Emilia in 1912 as a champion of the more violent group in the Socialist party. He was described at this time by one of the party as, 'a wonderful young man, spare of figure, hard, fiery, most original, with occasional bursts of eloquence; a man with a great future before him. You will see that he is destined to dominate the party.'

Editor and Soldier 1912–17

The split in the Socialist party between the moderates and the more violent groups gave Mussolini a chance to shine. Soon he was able to influence a wider field as he became editor of the Socialist paper *Avanti*. This was a paper with a national circulation and Mussolini soon increased its circulation. He moved into a flat in Milan with Rachele and their small daughter and he worked tremendously hard. He said that 'he worked like a dog'. *Avanti* encouraged the growing violence of the socialist demonstrations in Italy while Mussolini's reputation grew. However, he failed to gain a seat as Socialist candidate for Forli in 1913.

Upon the outbreak of war in 1914 Mussolini took the view of many Socialists that the proletariat had nothing to do with such a war. Italian intervention in the war must be the signal for revolution. However, the battle of the Marne showed that Germany was not going to win the war quickly. The King of Italy and some of his ministers began to feel that Italy might gain from taking part in the war. Mussolini also changed his views to suit the altered circumstances of a long grinding war.

He was growing tired of the strait-jacket of the Socialist control of *Avanti* and he began to think of starting his own newspaper. The French were keen that Italy should enter the war on the allied side and there is considerable evidence that Mussolini's new paper *Popolo d'Italia* was financed by the French when it started. Thus Mussolini's own Socialist daily was born. In the headings of the paper were two maxims: 'Who has steel has bread', and, 'Revolution is an idea which has found bayonets.' The new editor had borrowed his views from Blanqui, a French Socialist writer who put forward the idea of a government run by the workers using force if necessary, and also from Napoleon. In his first leading article, headed 'Audacity', Mussolini called on 'the young men of Italy' to go to war. Socialists regarded this warlike attitude as traitorous and he was expelled from the party with much bitter feeling on both sides.

Issue after issue of *Popolo d'Italia* came out in favour of entering the war and Mussolini formed groups of young men to organize demonstrations in Milan. These groups were termed *Fasci di Combattimento* and are the true forerunners of the Fascist party. *Fasci* was a Sicilian word used to describe a group. The link with Rome and the *fasces* or bundle of rods carried by the lictors was embroidery added at a later date.

Mussolini and Italy

With a journalist's instinct Mussolini had hit upon a good cause, Italian nationalism. Also the government of Italy was negotiating the Treaty of London which would bring them into the war on the Allied side against Austria with whom earlier negotiations had failed.

Mussolini when a soldier in the First World War

In August 1915 Mussolini was called up and posted to the 11th Bersaglieri. His war experience was confined to the trenches. Conditions were grim but he proved a good soldier and was promoted corporal and later lance-sergeant. He was not involved in any major battle but in 1917 he was wounded by the accidental explosion of a grenade in his trench during a demonstration. The barrel of the grenade-thrower had grown red-hot when the lieutenant in charge ordered the last two grenades to be fired. Mussolini dropped a grenade down the barrel and the thrower exploded. He claimed that 'forty-four splinters' entered his body and he wrote, 'I am proud to have reddened the road to Trieste with my own blood'. He was discharged from the army after a spell in hospital and he returned to his office leaning on crutches.

Pacifism in Italy was growing. Many were tired of the long period of trench warfare and the defeat at Caporetto in October 1917 encouraged the neutralists. However, in face of defeat the Italians began to rally and Mussolini's newspaper articles spurred them on while the *Fasci* dealt with pacifists in Milan. The Allies strengthened the Italian front and the Italian army recovered to play its part in the final defeat of the Central Powers.

With victory came the problems of government after the war and Mussolini's problem of how he was to satisfy his ambitions. He had learnt how to play upon popular feeling. He had changed his views on most subjects to fit the mood of the time. He had dropped his early pacifism and become an enthusiastic soldier. The ambitious young agitator with his burning sense of the injustice of the world had become the experienced journalist with a considerable following. The Italian people were discontented after the war and Mussolini was ready to use this discontent for his own advancement. He had already learnt the power of propaganda and the effectiveness of organized groups of followers. In the period immediately after the war he was shown by D'Annunzio in Fiume the way in which he could surround his actions with a popular appeal.

4   The Road to Power

D'Annunzio and Fiume

On the night of 11 September 1919 a motley band of men marched from Ronchi to Fiume. They were dressed in assorted uniforms but the black shirt of the Italian *arditi* (shock troops) was predominant. Leading this dark column through the night was a colourful figure, the poet D'Annunzio. Bald, one-eyed and virtually bankrupt, he still had a romantic charm. He had written some stirring war poems and had served Italy during the war in the cavalry, the infantry, the navy and finally the air service. In the latter he had won a reputation for daring which had cost him his eye. Like so many Italians after the war D'Annunzio had grown disillusioned and he felt that Italy had been betrayed by politicians. He attacked President Wilson of the U.S.A. and the members of the peace conference in a series of articles, and chose as the symbol of Italian wrongs the port of Fiume.

Fiume had been occupied by a small force made up of American, French and British troops in 1918. The Italians had also landed troops and their commander claimed the control of Fiume. The Italian flag flew over the city and there were a number of incidents. Some French troops were killed in the summer of 1919 and an international commission was sent out to Fiume. They decided that Fiume should be under international control. At this point D'Annunzio and his band arrived to claim the city.

For over a year D'Annunzio ruled over Fiume. The Italian government were prepared to leave him alone and they even helped him for a time. No other power was vitally interested. Though *The Times* reported all the happenings in Fiume, the world remained largely disinterested. Thus Fiume saw the first use of all the trappings of Fascism. The uniforms, the speeches, the bullying of opponents by forcing them to drink pints of castor oil, even the future Fascist war cry, were all used. D'Annunzio would appear on a balcony and work upon the crowd or the parade. He would end his speech with the formula: 'Whose is Fiume?' The answer crashed back, 'Ours'. 'To whom the future?' 'To us.' Then the troops present would raise their daggers and shout their cry: 'Ayah, ayah, alala!'

Schoolboys ran away from home to join this hero of Fiume while his followers organized piracy to support their state. The whole venture has the appearance of a comic opera and many of D'Annunzio's gestures were vulgar and futile. He flew over Rome and dropped a chamber pot full of carrots on the parliament buildings to show his feelings about the Italian government.

As time passed the economic situation in Fiume grew worse. Parades and show did not help the population to eat and they grew tired of the regime. In 1920 the Italian government came to an agreement with Yugoslavia at Rapallo. They agreed that Fiume should become an independent city. Giolitti, the Italian prime minister, ordered an attack on the city and D'Annunzio fled claiming that he had been betrayed. Mussolini contented himself with pointing out that he supported D'Annunzio but at least Yugoslavia had not got the city so no further action was required. Mussolini had seen what an

Mussolini with D'Annunzio from whom 'he learnt a great deal'

organized minority could do aided by clever propaganda provided that it did not clash with the army. He learnt a great deal from D'Annunzio's dress rehearsal of a Fascist coup.

The Italian Political Scene 1919–21

While D'Annunzio postured in Fiume the government faced problems at home. The war had been expensive and had completely disrupted the Italian economy. Throughout 1919 the price of food rose and strikes were common. These problems were added to those which have been outlined in chapter one and were basically the same as those that faced most European countries after the disruption of the 1914–18 War. The Italian political scene was such that no party emerged to solve these problems. Orlando's war ministry fell in June 1919 and Nitti, a professor of economics, tried to establish a government by making use of the usual bargains to gain the support of some Socialists for his moderate government. No clear political programme emerged, and amidst strikes and uncertainty two new parties appeared on the political scene. In January 1919 a Sicilian priest, Sturzo, formed the *Popolare* party which was progressive and called for reform at home and the ideals of the League of Nations abroad. This party won 101 seats at the election held in November 1919. In February 1919 there were Communist demonstrations in Milan. As an answer the Fascist party was born when Mussolini decided to revive his *Fasci*. A meeting was held on 23 March 1919 in a hall in Milan, and about 145 men, mostly disillusioned soldiers, attended. This party had no clear programme save a belief in action of some sort. A programme calling for various reforms such as a minimum wage and a foreign policy worthy of a great power was published later in Mussolini's paper. The party failed to win a seat at the 1919 elections and Mussolini was defeated by a Socialist by 175,936 votes. The Socialists held a mock funeral in Milan and stopping outside Mussolini's house they invited him to attend the burial of his party.

Nitti's coalition failed and his successor was the veteran politician Giolitti. He also tried to hold a coalition together and so avoided policies which might arouse feeling. This was one of the reasons that D'Annunzio was able to defy the

Italian government for so long. The government avoided any action which might lose them support. Peasants who had seized land after the war were carefully left alone and in September 1920 workers seized some of the factories in the North. Giolitti bided his time while the red flag flew over the factories. He believed that Socialism would burn itself out anyway. Property owners were not so hopeful nor so patient and they began to enrol armed bands of retainers to protect their belongings and to encourage the Fascists.

The Election of 1921

Because his party offered action Mussolini gained from the weakness of the government and from the unrest in the country. Giolitti was searching for allies against the Socialists in 1921. The Vatican had turned against him because his government proposed to tax the bonds which were the main form of Church property at this time. As a result Giolitti decided to use Fascist support against the Socialists. He believed that he could easily dominate Mussolini and once in power again he would discard the tougher elements among the Fascists. He made a sad mistake and he must be held responsible for giving Mussolini another chance after the mock funeral of his party. During the 1921 election the government used Fascist support to unseat Socialist and Catholic deputies. The Fascists beat up opponents. The police and prefects remained

'The Fascists beat up opponents'. A group of Blackshirts

neutral or actively aided them with transport and arms. Thirty-five Fascists were elected out of a total of 535 seats. Mussolini was elected at Milan and took his seat as the leader of a party which was only noted for its disorderly behaviour. The Italian political system in the hands of a manipulator like Giolitti had given the Fascists a chance to become an accepted political force.

Mussolini in Parliament 1921–22

Giolitti failed to hold his coalition together. Mussolini wasted no time in sitting with the opposition. The wind blew 'and these leaves which call themselves deputies will be blown about and mixed up anew'. Giolitti gave way to Bonorni and he, in his turn, gave way to Facta. None of them were able to build up a stable government. Mussolini was trying to establish his party politically while his followers ran riot throughout the country. Local leaders, calling themselves *ras*, which was the name of Ethiopian tribal chieftains, caused havoc. Balbo was a typical leader of this sort. He hated politics and the politicians, who, he believed, had betrayed Italy. He organized operations in the North and on 12 May 1922 he and 63,000 Fascists took over Ferrara. They only agreed to leave when the government promised to carry out a scheme of public works there. Mussolini was terrified that the government would use troops against such actions and he was constantly trying to restrain men like Balbo, while trying to keep their support for his political plans.

On 1 August 1922 the Socialists proclaimed a general strike as a protest against Balbo's actions in Romagna. This played into Mussolini's hands for he could offer to break the strike when the government did nothing. He could appear as the man to restore order while making use of his disorderly supporters. The strike collapsed after a day and Mussolini and his Fascists gained increasing support. In spite of the behaviour of the bands of blackshirts people began to feel that the Fascists might bring a return to order.

The army was loyal to the King. Victor Emmanuel III was afraid that he might be deposed by the Fascists and he feared a civil war. As a result he made no effort to co-operate with the government against the growing movement; a movement which was supported by many property owners who feared disorder and Communism, and which had been used by the government itself in 1921 in its effort to win the elections.

The March on Rome 1922

Government had virtually broken down by October 1922. People were sent to Mussolini for safe conduct passes with which to cross the country, and the situation was getting out of hand. Facta suggested that the entire cabinet should resign and when this idea was turned down by his colleagues he began to think in terms of a coalition with the Fascists. The troops were still loyal to the King and there can be little doubt that a firm government could have crushed any armed attempt to destroy the regime. Mussolini was well aware of this and he concentrated on political manœuvre. On his way to the Party Congress in Naples he spent a few hours in Rome and made known his demand for five portfolios in any new government.

Before leaving for the Party Congress Mussolini and his immediate followers had laid plans for military action. Now on his way through Rome Mussolini had seen for himself that the Facta government was helpless and thinking in terms of a coalition. At Naples he was further encouraged by the enthusiasm of his followers. Blackshirts were everywhere and the cry, ' *A Roma* ', was raised whenever a Fascist leader ended a speech. Mussolini fell in with the general mood and made an aggressive speech. He pointed out that the Fascists were not prepared to enter the government by the tradesman's entrance. The legions were ready to march.

'But I assure you in all solemnity that the hour has struck. Either they give us the government or we shall take it by falling on Rome.'

In the evening after the parades and speeches, Mussolini met the leaders of the various Fascist groups. Action was planned for 28 October on lines that had been worked out earlier. The Fascists were to concentrate at three points near Rome and then enter the city. The three concentration points were Civitavecchia, Tivoli and Monterotondo, and the groups were to reach these by any means of transport and so avoid the chance of an early clash with the army. Such a clash was to be avoided at all costs and army units were to be treated with courtesy and friendliness. The demand that was to be made to the government was simple. There must be a new cabinet with at least six Fascist ministers in important posts. The crowds in Naples cheered, the blackshirts paraded, and the general in charge of the troops in the area assured Mussolini of the support of his soldiers. On 25 October Mussolini left for Milan while the Party Congress continued to distract the government's attention.

The Facta cabinet moved slowly. They were convinced that they had plenty of time. The Fascists had not marched from Naples and so they must be ready to come to terms. The answer would be a new coalition which would include a number of Fascists. Confusion reigned as the members of the cabinet schemed. Facta decided to resign though his cabinet still ran the government until a new leader could be chosen. In view of this resignation the Fascist leaders hesitated as to whether or not their plans should go ahead for 28 October. The party machine could not be halted and local units began to requisition trains and to borrow arms from friendly military units. The trains began to roll towards the concentration points outside Rome early on 28 October.

Facta was persuaded to return and to declare a state of siege in Rome. He was reluctant to take such action but he went to the King to ask for a proclamation declaring a state of emergency. This would mean that the army would be called out against the Fascist columns. The King feared civil war and doubted Facta's ability to control the situation. He refused to sign the proclamation though he was approached twice.

Mussolini now knew that there would not be an armed clash and so he could afford to increase his demands. In his last article as editor he wrote in *Popolo d'Italia*: 'A tremendous victory is in sight with the almost unanimous approval of the nation. But victory is not to be mutilated by eleventh hour combinations. . . . The government must have a clear Fascist character.'

On 29 October Rachele Mussolini received a telephone message from Rome. Benito was wanted at the palace. About noon a telegram arrived confirming the telephone message.

Mussolini was to form a government and he was soon on his way to Rome flaunting his black shirt and determined that 'everything would function perfectly' and that the trains would run to time from then on.

Mussolini formed his government headed by a moderate cabinet containing only four Fascist ministers. He was secure in the knowledge that the nation was relieved at having a government prepared to act. In addition he knew that he had the support of the King, the army, and the industrialists as well as the loyalty of his Fascist followers.

The Fascist columns did not move on Rome until Mussolini had become prime minister. They then paraded in Rome and were received by the King before taking trains for home. Mussolini organized this dispersal and the last of his cheering legions left Rome on 31 October. Their leader had now to tackle the problem of government.

5 The Fascist Prime Minister

Early Success, 1922

From the start of his ministry Mussolini was determined that he should create a good impression as the moderate young leader who was determined to clean up Italian politics and restore the prestige of Italy abroad. On his way to the Lausanne Conference on Turkey his train stopped frequently so that he could address the enthusiastic crowds. At Lausanne he took care that a formal announcement should be made that Italy was to be treated as an equal. Curzon for Britain and Poincaré for France agreed to this and Mussolini played a small part in the proceedings from then on. Nevertheless the Italian press claimed that Mussolini was putting Italy on the map again. Shortly after this Mussolini made his only visit to London for a conference. He disliked the weather and the dirt and hurried home as soon as he could.

There he claimed in the chamber of deputies that he would work within the constitution. 'I might have made this bleak hall a bivouac for my platoons. I might have closed parliament altogether and created a government of Fascists alone. I could have done that, but such, at least for the present, has not been my wish.'

Impressed by this moderation the chamber and later the senate voted Mussolini full powers to reform the government. Mussolini then decided to make a tour of the country and to recruit a new national militia which should be drawn from the existing Fascist formations. His next step was to bring forward a new electoral law. He could not continue with only thirty-five Fascists in the chamber. The new law gave two-thirds of the seats in the chamber of deputies to the party that received the greatest number of votes over the country. The King refused to issue this law by decree so Mussolini had to try to get it through parliament. After a careful speech in which he

Mussolini and his bodyguard, December 1922

pointed out that the law was intended to produce stable government he put the new law to the vote. The result was a triumph, for both houses carried the law by over 100 votes.

Mussolini now felt that he must create a favourable situation in which to go to the country. Abroad he took a firm line. A boundary commission set up by the conference of Ambassadors ran into trouble on Greek territory near the Albanian frontier. An Italian general and all the other Italian members of the group were killed. Mussolini acted at once without waiting for full information about the incident. He sent a stiff note to the Greek government demanding a full apology and compensation amounting to 50 million lire. The Greeks refused and claimed that the League should investigate. The Italian navy bombarded Corfu and Italian marines landed on the island.

The Conference of Ambassadors in Paris, who had remained in being to deal with the details of the peace settlement after the 1914–18 War, took the matter from the League who were unable to come to any agreement with Mussolini. The Conference put pressure on the Greeks to accept modified terms which included an apology by the Greeks to the Powers and an indemnity to be paid if a commission found evidence to support Italian claims. By 27 September Italy received 50 million lire and withdrew her troops from Corfu. This was a triumph for Mussolini which the Italian press were quick to trumpet abroad, conveniently forgetting the part played by the Conference of Ambassadors. In addition Mussolini was able to come to an agreement with Yugoslavia by which Italy gained Fiume in return for certain concessions. At last D'Annunzio had been justified and the King showed his pleasure by giving Mussolini the title, 'Cousin to the Sovereign'.

Early in 1924 Mussolini went to the country and the Fascists polled over $4\frac{1}{2}$ million votes against nearly 3 million for all the other parties. Under the new electoral law the Fascists received 355 seats and Mussolini could feel secure. He overlooked the fact that some of his more zealous supporters had resorted to violent methods of persuasion during the elections.

The Murder of Matteoti

During the first few days of June 1924 a large seven-seater Lancia was seen in the area of the house of the Socialist deputy, Matteoti. Matteoti had been particularly outspoken in his criticism of Mussolini and his Fascist party. About 4 p.m. on 10 June Matteoti came out of his house on his way to parliament. He was carrying a bundle of papers and he hardly glanced at the men standing by the large car. Suddenly he was seized and in spite of a sturdy fight he was carried into the car which was driven off at great speed. The struggle continued in the car and a bystander took the number and informed the police. The car and its owners were traced but there was no sign of Matteoti. At some point during the struggle in the car he was stabbed to death. His body was not found until the middle of August when it was discovered in a shallow grave about twelve miles from Rome.

Matteoti's disappearance caused an outcry in Italy and the world. Mussolini and his supporters were accused of his abduction and then of his death. Like Henry II of England, who had gained from the murder of Archbishop Becket in 1170, Mussolini could claim that he had no direct responsibility for

Matteoti, the Socialist deputy who had been 'particularly out-spoken in his criticism of Mussolini'

the murder, though he had been angered by Matteoti's opposition. After the final trial in 1947 there can be no doubt that the abduction and murder were carried out by Fascists hoping to intimidate opposition. Mussolini's position was badly shaken and he was at a loss what to do.

Force must be the Solution

Mussolini ordered an investigation to take place into what had happened to the missing deputy. This started under upright judges though a second trial took place under Fascist authorities in 1925. The body of Matteoti was discovered during the investigation and the trial took on a very serious aspect.

31

Fortunately for Mussolini the opposition failed to exploit the situation. The Socialists withdrew, as the Romen plebs had done, from the chamber. [The Roman plebs had withdrawn to the Aventine Hill in protest against the aristocracy and the Socialists decided to use a similar means of protest against the Fascists.] This Aventine withdrawal received a good deal of support but it strengthened Mussolini's position in the chamber. He began to gain confidence in spite of the hostile groups outside his home. He issued a decree which gave local authorities the power to suppress newspapers. A memorial to Matteoti in the *Mondo* accused Mussolini of the responsibility for the murder. Such articles could be stopped and the leaders of the Fascists encouraged Mussolini to take even firmer action. The Fascist militia pledged their support and Fascist rallies were held all over Italy.

At the beginning of 1925 Mussolini spoke out: 'Italy wants peace and quiet, work and calm. I will give these things with love if possible and with force if necessary.' The chamber, without the members of the Socialist opposition cheered enthusiastically and Mussolini's confidence returned. The time for action had come. Mussolini was now determined to go with his party and to set up a state in which he would not be troubled by parliamentary opposition. His days as a parliamentary leader were over.

6 Early Years of the Fascist State

Mussolini's Machinery of Government

Forty-eight hours after his speech promising action Mussolini had started to build a dictatorship. The opposition was weak and divided, so Mussolini met little difficulty. The Aventine groups of deputies decided to remain away from the chamber. The King, when approached by some of the opposition, refused to dismiss Mussolini for fear of anarchy. The Fascist militia acted swiftly. Opposition clubs and offices were closed, houses were searched, and newspapers taken over. Known and outspoken opponents of Fascism were forced to eat a live toad, or they were given the Fascist baptism—a pint or two of castor oil to purge them from the sin of opposition.

The press was carefully censored. As a journalist, Mussolini was well aware of the importance of controlling the newspapers. The liberal *Corriere della Sera* was a famous paper which opposed Fascist action. The director of the paper was dismissed and the company which owned the paper was broken up. The paper was then taken over by the Fascists.

Mussolini was helped in such actions by the carefully fostered alarm at four attempts on his life. In November 1925 Zaniboni, a Freemason and a Socialist, attempted to kill Mussolini. His arrest gave the Fascists a chance to occupy Masonic lodges and to dissolve the Socialist Unitary party. In April 1926, Miss Violet Gibson, an Irishwoman, came to Rome determined to shoot either the Pope or Mussolini. By chance Mussolini was her first target and she hit him in the nose with her first pistol shot. She fired at point-blank range and it was fortunate for Mussolini that he had cultivated the habit of throwing his head back and sticking his chin out when he emerged into public. Mussolini behaved calmly on this occasion and gained the utmost from this attack by an unbalanced Irishwoman. He was bandaged and then called out to the bystanders: 'If I go forward, follow me. If I go back, kill me. If I die, avenge me.' The press made much of the incident and Mussolini generously allowed the release of Miss Gibson. Two further attempts were made on Mussolini's life in 1926 and he made use of both to underline the belief that Italy would be ruined without his care and Fascist control.

The government was brought completely under Mussolini's control. In the local districts elected mayors were replaced by nominated officials. In the central government the prime minister became the head of state responsible to the King alone. The head of state, Mussolini, was able to choose his own ministers without reference to anybody. Later, in 1928, the King was shorn of his last power. He was no longer allowed to choose the head of state's successor. This was to be done by the Fascist Grand Council. In January 1926 a law was passed by the subservient parliament in which many members wore the black shirt. This gave Mussolini the power to issue decrees which were to have the full force of law. Over 100,000 decrees were to be issued while Mussolini was in power.

The system by which the government was elected was arranged so that a hollow shell of democracy remained. Lists were drawn up by the unions of employees and workers and from these the Fascist Grand Council chose a list of parliamentary candidates. This list could either be accepted or rejected by the electorate. They were left no real choice. In 1929 and 1934 there were elections and the official lists were accepted by the people. The old parliament was eventually replaced by a nominated chamber of fasces and corporations in 1939. The chamber would cheer whenever Mussolini appeared on the scene. Then they would burst into the Fascist song, '*Giovinezza*'. Parliament had become a mere rubber stamp which Mussolini chose to use to show the popularity of his regime.

The Party

As well as being head of state Mussolini was also the Duce of the Fascist party. He was particularly proud of the way in which he fitted the Fascist party into the State. A system of twin beds as he liked to call it. In fact the system was clumsy and all too often one branch of the government issued orders which were opposite to those issued by another branch. The Duce acted as umpire and often contradicted his own orders shortly after they had been issued. The party itself was headed by the Duce, who chose the party secretary. The party secretary nominated the party directorate which met weekly. He also nominated the ninety-two provincial secretaries who met together once or twice a year in the National Council. The party secretary was also secretary of the Grand Council of Fascism. Mussolini alone could call the Grand Council and he decided on its agenda and its membership. He used the twenty-two members of the Grand Council to check any powerful group within the party or the cabinet. With a system like this where departments were not clearly defined Mussolini was able to play groups off against each other. He took care that no rival should appear.

In February 1925 Farinacci became secretary of the Fascist party. He was a tough product of the early years of Fascism and he took care that the independence of the local bosses or *ras* was checked. He carefully centralized the whole system and destroyed any local independence. Mussolini took care that no party secretary grew too powerful. They changed almost yearly and only Starace, 1931–39, lasted for any length of time. An indication of the lack of able men in the Fascist party was shown by the fact that in 1941 Vidussoni became party secretary. His only qualifications were that he was young. He was a cheerful aide-de-camp type aged twenty-eight who had won a medal during the Spanish Civil War. Able men were not encouraged in a system which depended so much on Mussolini's whim.

Membership of the party fluctuated. At first the party card was restricted and only issued to carefully chosen people. Then it became an essential document in certain professions. In 1932 civil servants, teachers, and army officers had to be members of the Fascist party. In 1940 the party membership was thrown open to all members of the armed forces. One group alone remained at the top of the party and enjoyed special privileges. This group was made up of those who had joined the party before 1922; those who had taken part in the March on Rome; those who had remained loyal during the Matteoti crises. This

35

RETTORATO
AULA MAGNA
BIBLIOTECA

CREDERE OBBEDIRE COMBATTERE

Mussolini takes the salute during a ceremony at which University students were sworn into the army. In front of the Duce a huge book displays the oath used

group was the tough centre of the early Fascist movement and they remained in control. No new generation came to their place for young men were not encouraged to shine. As time passed Mussolini found that all his government changes were a mere changing of the guard.

Fascism and the Italians

To many Italians the Fascist government itself was just a new guard. Their life was hard and centred upon the seasons. Poor harvests meant hunger and starvation and the thin soil of most of Italy seldom produced much of a harvest. The hardworking peasants resented government interference of any sort and resented paying taxes of all sorts. The Fascists were just another government and were distrusted in spite of promises of better things to come. When the Fascists proved oppressive most citizens simply sought their own salvation regardless of their fellows. Ignazio Silone in his novel *Fontamara* describes the return of a group of peasants who find the village square full of blackshirts. Of these the narrator says:

'If you met them in the street in daytime they would be humble and fawning. By night and in numbers they were wicked and evil. They have always been at the disposal of anyone who gives orders, and they always will be. But recruiting them into a special army, giving them a special uniform and special arms, is something new and peculiar to the last few years.

'Such are the so-called Fascists.

'Their boldness had another explanation, too. Each of us would have been a match for at least three of them. But what chance had we in their midst? What was there to bind us together? What link was there between us?

'There we all were in the middle of the square. We were all born at Fontamara. That was the only thing we had in common. Every one of us thought first of himself. Everyone tried to think of the best way of getting out of that square of armed men and leaving the others behind. Every one of us had a family, and we all thought of our families.'

Once the Fascists were in power most Italians accepted their government. It was safer to do so and, after all, the Fascists carefully pointed out that their rule brought efficiency and international prestige.

The 'Napoleonic' Legislation and the Corporative State

During 1925 and 1926 Mussolini issued a mass of decrees to strengthen his new Fascist government. Any civil servant who showed independence was dismissed. Newspaper owners were held responsible for editorial policy and found that Fascist views were safest. Mussolini regarded 1926 as his Napoleonic year and he considered the corporative state as his great constructive achievement. This untidy piece of organization was never fully followed through. It was based on the Fascist concept of the importance of the State. Every citizen must exist for the State and work as a cog in the great machine of the State. Employers and workers were to be organized in unions or corporations so that the minister of corporations could control the economic life of the country. In order to bring this about Mussolini issued a series of decrees which set up a number of corporations for every profession and branch of industry based on a scheme outlined in the Labour Charter of 1927. In 1936 there were twenty-two groups of citizens ranging from the fifth group which was made up of those working in the sugar and beet industry to the twenty-second group which was made up of the professional classes and artists. Members of the corporations paid their dues and took their orders from appointed officials. Any dispute over wages or conditions was settled by the officials. The National Council of Corporations was in charge of the general policy throughout the various industries. Posts for Fascists could be found in this system which became notoriously corrupt and inefficient in action, though it appeared impressive on paper. Taps were put into buildings and never connected to the water supply because the money for the pipes had gone into the pockets of members of the party. Mussolini produced this system and managed by clever propaganda to mask the fact that it was not really connected up and running.

The Lateran Treaty 1929

While creating the Fascist state Mussolini had been secretly trying to reach an agreement with the Roman Catholic Church. The argument over the rights and the position of the Pope in Italy still divided the country. Mussolini was to receive general acclaim when he brought about a solution by the agreement with Pope Pius XI. Mussolini began by restoring the crucifix in schools and law courts and by proposing a revision of ecclesiastical legislation. Late in 1925 he was married to Rachele in a Milanese church as a gesture to placate the Vatican. Pius XI was prepared to negotiate but there was reluctance and hostility from the rank and file on both sides. Members of the Fascist party attacked religious establishments and did considerable damage. This made Mussolini's position difficult. He grew angry when he was reminded that he had written a novel called *The Cardinal's Mistress* in his early years. Negotiations continued between Mussolini and Cardinal Gasparri and eventually agreement

Cardinal Gasparri signs the treaty and concordat under Mussolini's watchful gaze

was reached. A treaty and a concordat were signed on 11 February 1929 at the Lateran, the papal cathedral. The Pope recognized the Kingdom of Italy under the House of Savoy and Italy recognized the independence of the Holy See. The Pope received the Vatican City where he was in fact living. This small area within the city of Rome was to be under the Pope's control. The Vatican City had its own army, police force, courts, prison, radio station, post office, and newspaper. The Roman Catholic Church was confirmed as the State Church in Italy with the right to claim government protection. In return for giving up all other papal claims over Italian territory the Church received 750 million lire in cash and 1,000 million lire in government bonds.

The news of this agreement was greeted with enthusiasm throughout Italy and the world. Italians felt happy that their Church had come to terms with their Duce. The deep wound caused in 1870 when the Pope had refused to recognize the Italian government could now be healed. Of course the Pope and Mussolini failed to agree for long on matters of state policy. To the delight of his followers Mussolini refused to kneel and kiss the Pope's hand on his first official visit to the Vatican after the agreement had been signed. The State was not going to be the servant of the Church. Later Mussolini was to have a spirited battle with the Pope over the part played in the State by Catholic Action, an organization set up to encourage social work by Catholics. The Pope could be an outspoken critic of the Fascists as his encyclical of 1931 proved. Nevertheless Mussolini and the Pope never really endangered the agreement of 1929 and Mussolini regarded this as one of his greatest achievements. He was proud that this wound had been healed and he was proud of the apparent strength of the Fascist state. The party emblem, the lictor's *fasces*, was now superimposed on the state coat of arms and the party anthem, '*Giovinezza*' was heard everywhere.

The Fascist party emblem, the lictor's *fasces*

7 The Dictator

At this point it is worth taking a closer look at Mussolini and the way in which he worked. He had become dictator of Italy through a mixture of clever publicity and tough organization. Now that he had reached the position of dictator his character and his methods were to have an influence on Italian life and European affairs.

Mussolini and his family. From the left Rachele holding Anna Maria, Romano held by Mussolini, Edda, Bruno, Vittorio

Mussolini was short, about five foot six inches, and he was strongly built. He took a great deal of exercise in an effort to keep himself fit. He fenced, boxed, rode, and swam with vigour. His hair was receding from his great forehead but this tended to emphasize the rolling eyes which were his most striking physical feature. His voice was musical and many people have written of the effectiveness of Mussolini's public speeches. His impact on visitors was considerable and Winston Churchill was one of those who were favourably impressed by the Duce. Franz von Papen wrote of Mussolini in 1933:

'I found the Italian dictator a man of very different calibre to Hitler, short in stature, but with an air of great authority, his massive head conveyed an impression of great strength of character. He handled people like a man who was accustomed to having his orders obeyed, but displayed immense charm and did not give the impression of a revolutionary.'

Von Papen went on to say that he felt that Mussolini would be a good influence on Hitler.

Mussolini, 'the man of action'

Mussolini was always trying to prove himself and he suffered from a basic uncertainty of his own ability. He covered this by his pose of being the man of action and swift decision. His numerous passing affairs with women underline this. He was always showing off and loved to quote from a knowledge picked up from his superficial and speedy reading. His ignorance on most matters of government was in fact very great. He never admitted to this lack of knowledge and preferred to do without a German interpreter rather than show his lack of fluency in the German language. He knew little of economics and never bothered to find out the real state of the armed forces in Italy. Another country's political system merely bored Mussolini. His programme was simply one of action. Action which would prove his greatness and show Italian power. The papers were always full of action pictures showing the Italian people the example set by their active and energetic leader.

The Duce's daily life was simple. For a time he lived in a small rented flat before moving to the Villa Torlonia. At this larger house surrounded by twenty acres of land he was able to make use of a tennis court and a riding track. Pictures of him riding round this track were taken at an angle which made the small hurdles appear quite large jumps. Even in these surroundings Mussolini's life was simple. A gastric ulcer in 1925 confirmed him in his frugal eating habits. He ate little and never spent more than a few minutes over his meals. Fruit, bread and coffee made up his breakfast. Spaghetti, vegetables and clear soup were his staple diet at other meals. He neither smoked nor drank spirits. He would sometimes drink a glass of wine or orangeade. He always went to bed early and would sleep soundly while the light in his office was left burning to show how he worked for his people.

Mussolini went out to official functions very little and, when he did, he was careful to behave correctly. He had a young man from the foreign office, Pansa, to teach him English and social deportment. Pansa persuaded Mussolini to give up wearing the spats of which he had grown so fond. At times there were social disasters as when Mussolini used his fish knife to shovel his food into his mouth. But he learnt quickly and the Dictator made few social blunders. He

43

Pictures were taken 'which made the small hurdles appear quite large jumps'

took care to wear correct formal clothes on official occasions.

At work Mussolini ran the government in rather the same way as a busy editor might run a large newspaper. In 1929 the government offices were moved into the Palazzo Venezia. Mussolini's own office was a large room on the second floor which had a balcony looking out over the square below. This room was called the *Sala del Mappamondo* after an ancient map of the world which hung there. The room was over sixty feet long and forty feet wide and it was two stories high. The only furniture was a desk beside a huge ornate fireplace. Visitors were always impressed when they entered this vast room with the Duce seated at work in one corner of it.

On a normal morning when he was in Rome Mussolini would start work in his huge office about eight. He would see the head of the secret police, the foreign minister, the minister who controlled the press, the secretary of the party, and other officials. A mass of reports would be brought to him and he would read them and initial them in blue pencil with the letter 'M'. He never made comment and most decisions were taken verbally or over the telephone. Obviously such a system made any careful planning and discussion impossible. In fact there was little discussion on policy. The council of ministers

The Sala del Mappamondo

was a body of subordinates and the Fascist Grand Council only met when Mussolini wished. No records were kept of the meetings and Mussolini would stray from the agenda as he tested the reactions of the meetings to his various schemes. Major moves in policy were announced to the people from the balcony of the Palazzo Venezia. They would then be given full and careful press coverage. Mussolini's speeches from the Palazzo Venezia were greeted with enthusiasm by the crowds. He knew how to handle the crowd and many of them were filled with genuine enthusiasm though some unwilling members of the Fascist party appeared because they had received a red postcard which ordered them to attend the meeting.

Such a system of government was very personal and was bound to become cut off from reality. Mussolini only met party members who were his subordinates. He met no criticism, and independent action by his followers was regarded as disloyal and dangerous. The Minister of Education, Bottai, wrote of Mussolini in the period after 1935: 'The Church, the King, the mob, Starace and the party, were as convinced as he was that he could make no mistakes. My friends and I, who were his only real friends, offered him advice still, and we were subsequently proved to be right. But by then it was too

45

'Mussolini would start work in his huge office about eight'

late. Advice bounced off him and came back at us like a boomerang, in the form of epigrams and mottoes.'

Much of Mussolini's time was spent dealing with propaganda and this also made him lose sight of the real issues. Italy could not afford an ambitious foreign policy but Mussolini characteristically wished his country to have one. He was in a position in which he could start to bring about such a policy and this was to lead to his ruin. He blamed the Italian people for the failure and said: 'It is the material I lack. Even Michelangelo had need of marble to make statues. If he had only had clay he would have been nothing more than a potter.' As the Dictator of Italy Mussolini tried to fashion the marble statue of a first-class power from the clay of the resources of a minor power.

8 Fascism Triumphant

'Mussolini is always right.' [Fascist slogan]

Mussolini took care to create the image of the efficient Fascist state. Some of his propaganda appears ludicrous but he knew that if something is stated often enough and loud enough it will usually stick in the mind. Especially if it is stated in a neat slogan or jingle. His system had to appear to be efficient and powerful. The appearance of power mattered more than the reality. To question the Duce was made a matter of doubting the greatness of Italy. Active opposition led to the active answer of the Fascist baptism.

Most Italians accepted Mussolini's rule without much argument. Those who had allowed him to gain power found it impossible to unseat him. The King winced when he heard *'Giovinezza'* being played instead of the national anthem but he knew that he could not dismiss Mussolini without an active and united body of support. This support was not likely to appear while the Fascist government gave Italy strong government. As a journalist Mussolini knew the ways in which he could create the impression of the strong and efficient government which was his justification. It became increasingly difficult for anyone to learn the truth. Even Mussolini lost sight of reality. He claimed that Italy had no need of aircraft carriers because she was one vast natural aircraft carrier herself. This made a good slogan but Mussolini had no idea as to how many aircraft he had on the deck of his carrier.

Show was all-important and Mussolini altered his window dressing to suit the moment. Fascism had come to the fore with a vague programme promising action. Now the Fascist state triumphed and Mussolini issued a mass of slogans which were to prove how strong and efficient it was. The Fascist attitude towards any critic was summed up in the 'could not care less' attitude of their motto *'me ne frego'* (do not irritate me). The State was perfect and Mussolini wrote in the article on Fascism in the *Enciclopedia Italiana*: 'The Fascist conception

'Mussolini issued a mass of slogans'

of the State is all-embracing, and outside the state no human or spiritual values can exist...' Slogans were painted up everywhere: 'Better to live one day as a lion than a hundred years as a sheep.' Imperial Rome was used as an example of Italian greatness in the past. The lictor's *fasces* were adopted as the symbol of a party which had come into being as *fasci* or groups of thugs. An interest in archaeology, aided by the government, did result from this interest in Roman history, and a number of great excavations were begun.

Mussolini had to try to capture the imagination of Italian youth. The older generation might be dazzled by slogans and show but, if Fascism was to live, the younger generation must believe in it. Thus, although illiteracy was still a serious problem in Italy, Mussolini worried more about the teaching of Fascism in the schools than the problem of educating the mass of the Italian people. Out of 317 history textbooks which were in use in 1926, 101 were forbidden. By 1936 there was a single history textbook which was compulsory. 1922 was to be *anno primo* of a new era in the history of Italy. Words for spelling lessons were connected with fighting and the early readers were full of such sentences as: 'The eyes of the Duce are on every one of you.' 'How can we ever forget that Fascist boy

Balilla parade with their gasmasks

who, when near to death, asked that he might put on his uniform and that his savings should go to the party?'

At the age of four a child became a 'son of the she-wolf' and put on his first black shirt. At eight he joined the *Balilla* which was a group named after a Genoese boy who threw a stone at the Austrian troops in a rebellion of 1746. At fourteen young

Fascist girls parade enthusiastically

Italians joined the *Avanguardisti*. This system filled youth with the ideas of Fascism. Handshakes were not allowed because they indicated weakness. Good Fascists gave the Fascist salute. Unfortunately even Mussolini was inclined to forget this and shake hands with visitors.

Apart from education Mussolini concentrated on the press. He was happiest in the world of newspapers where he had been so successful. He took absurd care that his press image should be right. No mention was allowed of him falling off his horse. No mention was to be made of his fiftieth birthday for he wished to retain a youthful image. He always sorted the press photographs carefully so that only the most flattering should be released. The radio was in its infancy. A law of 1927 set up Radio Italiana but Mussolini found that this new means of communication did not suit him. He gave few radio talks, though all great occasions were broadcast. On the other hand Mussolini enjoyed films, especially comedies. He had private film shows nearly every evening and was determined to encourage the Italian film industry. He tried to restrict the number of foreign films shown in the country, but the Fascist films were dull and Italians preferred the technically superior American products.

Sport was also brought under the control of the State. Italians must succeed in this field to prove the superiority of Fascism. The Olympic Games Committee became a branch of the Fascist party. Boxing was, as Mussolini said, 'the Fascist

Mussolini inspecting tennis champions during a parade of 15,000 athletes

method of self-expression'. In 1933 Carnera became the world heavyweight champion. Much was made of this and the press were told never to show pictures of Carnera being knocked down. Italian players at lawn tennis matches were ordered to wear the black shirt and to give the Fascist salute. Football was brought under rigid central control and there was a chief referee in Rome with a gold whistle.

Persecution

Much of this seems absurd and harmless, but there was a harsh side to the Fascist regime. Those who would not conform were made to suffer. Fortunately the police system was not very efficient, but Italians were often made aware that they were living in a police state. Fascist courts were set up and there was no appeal from such bodies. The ordinary police, the *carabinieri*, were loyal to the King, but Mussolini had control of the Fascist militia and his special police. This body he named O.V.R.A. to frighten people. Nobody really knows what the letters stand for and much of the work of this force was made sterile by the fact that there were at least twenty divisions often working against each other. Still with such police control it did pay to conform, and many felt that such control was a fair price for the apparent efficiency of the government.

Many Italians left the country in disgust. Both Nitti and Sturzo were among the political leaders who did so. Many settled in Paris where Rosselli, who was later murdered by Mussolini's hired assassins, edited the anti-Fascist paper, *Justice and Liberty*. Three thousand, three hundred and fifty of these exiles fought on the Republican side in the Spanish Civil War when a Garibaldi brigade was formed in November 1936. A number of them were to return in 1943 to bring new life to a ruined country.

The Economic Front

It was typical of Mussolini's approach that economic problems should be regarded as a series of battles. When the impact of the American Wall Street crash was felt in Italy the Battle of the Lira was launched to save the national currency. The

United States recalled loans in an effort to steady their economy and as a result the Italian lira dropped in value. Mussolini was determined not to devalue the lira. Workers were ordered to take a cut in wages to fight for their nation's economy.

The Battle for Grain followed. This was an effort to reduce Italian import of wheat in a drive for economic self-sufficiency.

'The Battle for Grain'. Mussolini encourages the harvesters

Gold, silver or bronze stars were issued to successful farmers on 21 April each year. Mussolini was photographed driving a tractor or reaping in the fields. The production of wheat rose and imports were cut by 75 per cent in the ten years after 1925. This wheat production helped some farmers to grow rich on government subsidy but it upset Italian agriculture. Marginal land which would have been better used for growing fruit and olives was turned over to wheat. Also the cost of wheat to the consumer remained high because of the subsidy. The battle was won but it was won with no regard for the balance of the Italian economy.

Obvious signs of Mussolini's operations were the great land-reclamation schemes sponsored by the government. Large sums were set aside for land drainage until the money was

Mussolini driving a tractor during work on the Pontine marshes

needed for armaments after 1934. The draining of the Pontine marshes near Rome was a great technical achievement and one which was easily shown to visitors to the city. It was soon pointed out that Mussolini had succeeded where Caesar had failed. In Rome itself there were other indications of the activity of the Fascist government. Large buildings appeared and much of medieval Rome was swept away to make room for the new Rome of the new Empire. Government buildings, post offices, Fascist headquarters, the railway station, all showed Mussolini's passion for show by their sheer size.

53

Communications were improved. The mainline trains ran to time and new trunk roads, *autostrade*, were begun to link the main cities. The concentration was on the outward show rather than the essentials. Little interest was taken in the transport problems off the main routes. Mussolini was often pictured opening new roads and new buildings but there was no general sense of purpose. It was enough that the Fascists were getting things done. The aircraft industry was encouraged as a symbol of Italy's might. In 1927 and 1928 Major de Bernardi set world speed records in a Macchi seaplane powered by a Fiat motor. However, Italian aircraft production fell behind that of the other European powers as the war drew close in 1939.

The most energetic efforts were put into advertising Mussolini's campaign of the 'Battle for Births'. He felt that Italy's population of 40 million should be raised to 60 million by the middle of the twentieth century. A great country must produce great legions for its service. Mothers were therefore looked after as never before in Italy. Bachelors, except for clergy and disabled war veterans, were heavily taxed. Prizes were given for large families and in 1933 Mussolini personally congratulated ninety-three Italian mothers. Between them these women had borne 1,300 children. In spite of this campaign the birth rate fell. Mussolini was furious in 1932 when, for the first time since 1876, there were fewer than one million live births during the year.

Foreign Policy 1925–35

While attention was held by the great schemes of public works and the various campaigns on the home front Mussolini was content to rattle a sabre abroad rather than to draw it from its sheath. He had shown aggressive action over Corfu and he claimed to have gained Fiume. For the time being he was content to await events and see how much he could gain for Italy.

In 1925 negotiations were set in motion by Britain to arrange guarantees for the Franco-German and Belgo-German frontiers. Such guarantees were intended to increase the chance of a lasting peace in Europe. Mussolini showed his interest at once and demanded a guarantee of Italy's northern frontier. The German government pointed out that they would have to annex Austria if they were to guarantee the Brenner frontier. Mussolini sulked for a time and then decided at the last moment to attend the Locarno discussions. He took a special train from Rome to Milan, a racing car from Milan to Stresa and a speedboat from Stresa to Locarno. He was annoyed to find that his arrival was not greeted with any enthusiasm. He signed the guarantees of the German frontiers with France and Belgium in a thoroughly bad humour. He blamed the French for Italy's cool reception. In addition he knew that many Italian exiles were in France. As a result of this feeling he drew closer to Britain. An agreement was reached on the frontier between Egypt and Libya and there was talk of British support for an Italian railway over Ethiopia.

Mussolini's foreign policy was sometimes skilful in execution but he had no general purpose. He could impress foreign powers but had no firm plans for the future of Italy. He was only interested in the short-term gains which would bring prestige to his regime. Furthermore he refused to be guided by experts. He was jealous of any ability shown by his subordinates, and Grandi was sent as ambassador to London in 1932 because he was gaining a reputation as a skilful negotiator at the Geneva Disarmament Conference. When Grandi had been moved Mussolini became minister for foreign affairs himself. After ten years in power Mussolini could say: 'The twentieth century will be the century of Fascism. It will be the century of Italian power.'

Obviously his signature on the Kellogg Pact meant very little. The Kellogg Pact was drawn up by Senator Kellogg, the American secretary of state, and was signed by all major powers. The Pact 'condemned recourse to war for the solution of international disputes'. At one moment Mussolini could claim that Italy was the one stable element in Europe at another he claimed that Italy was a growing nation that needed to expand.

Then, on 30 January 1933, Hitler became Chancellor of the German Reich. Mussolini welcomed the arrival of a new Fascist leader though he feared a German challenge. In 1933 he suggested a four-power pact between Italy, France, Britain and Germany to keep the peace in Europe. France preferred to stick to the League and to her own alliances such as the Little Entente. Hitler was in favour of the alliance as was Ramsay MacDonald of Britain. However, the plan was not pushed through and was eventually signed by Germany and Italy alone.

Between Italy and Germany lay Austria, and there could be no doubt that Hitler had designs on his homeland. He used to emphasize this by showing visitors a view of Salzburg through a telescope set up at the Berghof. Italians were very touchy about the Brenner frontier and Mussolini watched carefully to make sure that Germany did not get away with anything. Hitler withdrew from the Disarmament Conference and the League of Nations. Mussolini promptly undertook Italian rearmament. He decided that he could gain most by balancing between the rising power of Germany on the one hand and the dormant powers, Britain and France, on the other.

It was in this atmosphere that Hitler first visited Italy. The meeting took place at Venice. Hitler was furious with his advisors because Mussolini was resplendent in uniform while

'Mussolini was resplendent in uniform' while Hitler was 'wearing his shabby civilian clothes'. Venice 1934

he was wearing his shabby civilian clothes. The two dictators talked at each other a great deal. Mussolini complained that Hitler would keep reciting *Mein Kampf*—'That boring book which I have never been able to read', he added. Hitler was impressed by Mussolini's control over the crowds and by his agreeable conversation. Both leaders misunderstood each other, largely because Mussolini insisted that he knew German so well that he did not need an interpreter.

The Austrians counted on Italian support against German action and Mussolini publicly declared that Italy would stand by the Austrian government. The Austrian Chancellor, Dollfuss, was a friend of Mussolini's and relied on his support. In July 1934 a group of Nazi toughs shot Dollfuss and left him in his office to die from the wounds. The Austrian government acted swiftly and the Nazi revolt in Austria was checked within a day. It was well known that the Austrian Nazis had been helped by the Germans and the world waited to see what would happen. Mussolini did not hesitate. Troops were sent to the frontier. Hitler backed down hastily and Mussolini's prestige grew.

DOGS OF PEACE?

ITALY. "NOW NONE OF YOUR SNIFFING ROUND HERE, MIND!"
GERMANY. "MY DEAR FELLOW, NOTHING WAS FURTHER FROM MY INTENTION."

9 Imperial Ambitions

'My objective is simple. I want to make Italy great, respected and feared.'

Mussolini

Abyssinia

A small item of news appeared in some of the London newspapers late in 1934. It stated that a strong body of Abyssinians had attacked an Italian outpost at Wal-Wal near the border of Italian Somaliland and Abyssinia. Nobody bothered about this incident which had occurred when the British mission studying grazing rights in the area had withdrawn. The Italians repulsed the attack but received considerable losses in the encounter. Mussolini saw in this incident a chance to revenge the Italian defeat at Adowa in 1896 and to build Italy's African empire. At the time Italy controlled Eritrea, Italian Somaliland and Libya. He decided to make the Emperor of Abyssinia give Italy great concessions and to use force if necessary. Speed was essential because Mussolini did not wish to leave his northern frontier undefended for too long in the face of Hitler's growing power. Military preparations were started at once, though the rainy season in Abyssinia meant that actual operations would have to wait until the autumn.

Mussolini felt that he had the support of Britain and France in this venture. After all he had saved Austria from Germany for them. Laval for France later claimed that he had only promised support for Italian economic action in Abyssinia when he had talked to Mussolini. The three powers, Britain, France and Italy met at Stresa in 1935 to condemn German action over the Austrian revolt. Eden for Britain was ill and unable to attend the meeting. Nobody else was prepared to tackle Mussolini on the question of his plans for Abyssinia. In view of his obvious military preparations Mussolini took this silence as meaning British consent.

There was a period of desperate negotiation to avoid war during the summer of 1935. Italian troops poured into Africa. Five regular divisions, five blackshirt divisions, two native divisions, and a substantial air force were placed under General De Bono's command. The muddled negotiations encouraged Mussolini to attack and he set the date for October 1935. The Emperor of Abyssinia appealed to the League of Nations.

At dawn on 3 October 1935 De Bono's forces crossed the Abyssinian frontier. Mussolini announced this action to the Italian people. In face of the immediate condemnation by the League of Nations he was able to whip up patriotic feeling. Married women came forward to give up their gold wedding rings to help the war effort.

The League had acted fast enough but not firmly enough. Italy were condemned as an aggressor and ships were forbidden to carry arms to Italy and any goods from Italy. There was no such embargo on oil, coal, iron and steel going to Italy and the Suez Canal was not closed to Italian warships and transports.

'The Awful Warning'
A 'Punch' cartoon that shows the Anglo-French inaction over the Italian invasion of Abyssinia

THE AWFUL WARNING.

FRANCE AND ENGLAND (*together?*). "WE DON'T WANT YOU TO FIGHT, BUT, BY JINGO, IF YOU DO, WE SHALL PROBABLY ISSUE A JOINT MEMORANDUM SUGGESTING A MILD DISAPPROVAL OF YOU."

Britain and France tried to save the day by negotiation. Sir Samuel Hoare, the British foreign secretary, and Laval, the French premier, drew up a plan by which the Italians would gain control of nearly two-thirds of Abyssinia. Public opinion in Britain was roused and such a concession was condemned. On 18 December 1935 Hoare resigned and the Hoare-Laval Pact was dead. Hitler watched this Anglo-French failure, the discomfiture of the League, and the separation of Italy from Britain and France, with great glee.

In Abyssinia De Bono advanced steadily using aircraft and gas bombs, which Vittorio Mussolini described as looking like a budding rose when they exploded, against the enemy forces and towns. Adowa was occupied by the Italians on 6 October 1935, and De Bono wished to consolidate his position. Mussolini wanted results in the face of hostile world opinion. The Fascist De Bono was promoted marshal and recalled, and the regular soldier Badoglio took his place. Badoglio did consolidate and, spurred on by Mussolini, he advanced with great efficiency into Abyssinia. The Italian engineers did particularly good work on the roads. In April 1936 a battle at Lake Ashangi meant the end of the Abyssinian army. The Emperor, Haile Selassie, fled and on 5 May Marshal Badoglio rode into Addis Ababa at the head of the Italian army. Mussolini was able to announce the creation of a new Italian empire. He had

Italian forces advance in Abyssinia

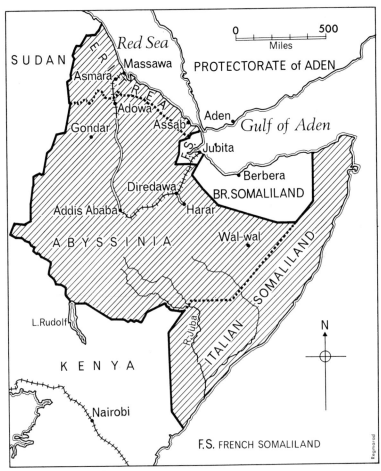

The new Italian empire

defied the world and gained an empire. He was triumphant
and it seemed that nothing could halt his plans to make Italy
great.

The Spanish War

'The Italian character has to be formed through fighting'
was one of Mussolini's maxims. The breach between Britain,
France and Italy gave Hitler his chance to move into the
Rhineland in March 1936. Nobody moved against him and

the German threat to Austria increased. Mussolini had vague hopes of rebuilding the Stresa front·in the face of this German threat to Austria. At the same time he was filled with the excitement brought on by his military success in Africa. He wanted another victory to add to his honours. The chance for military glory came in Spain and Mussolini used his forces there just when he should have been concentrating on preparing support for Austria.

In July 1936 General Franco began a military revolt against the Spanish Republican government. As early as 1934 the Spanish Fascists had approached the Italians for help. Now Franco asked Mussolini for twelve aircraft at once. These were sent on condition that they were used as escort planes only. Mussolini believed that Franco would win swiftly and so he felt that he must take part in the war soon if he was to gain glory for Italy. These early Italian pilots wore the uniform of the Foreign Legion but they were soon reinforced by volunteers from the Italian army.

Mussolini's policy of intervention in Spain was encouraged by his son-in-law, Ciano, whom he had appointed minister of foreign affairs in the summer of 1936. Ciano was a frivolous young man who spent much of his time on the golf course. He had to persuade Mussolini that golf was a Fascist game. Ciano was anti-British, which made it unlikely that British efforts to strengthen any Italian alliance would succeed. Ciano was able to keep one move ahead of the British government because he had a spy in the service of Lord Perth, the British ambassador to Rome. The spy had fitted a false back to Lord Perth's safe and in this way learnt of the British plans. Both Britain and France were members of the Non-Intervention Committee set up by the League of Nations in the face of the troubles in Spain. Both these countries were afraid that they would be drawn into war with Italy and Germany over Spain. As a result they did nothing to stop Franco from getting Italian help and the help of the German Condor Legion.

In a search for a quick and glorious victory Mussolini got drawn deeper into the Spanish struggle. At first the Italian troops were termed volunteers. The Italian press officials denied that there was any official intervention. Unfortunately they failed to censor a film which was shown in Rome. The film showed the Spanish Fascist forces taking Malaga and the audiences cheered at the sight. They laughed and cheered even louder when they noticed that the 'Spanish' forces rode in vehicles carrying the Italian War Office number plates. It became impossible to disguise the fact that nine battalions of Italian blackshirts in tanks and armoured cars had operated under their own commander, General Roatta, in the attack on Malaga early in 1937.

Mussolini became more and more reckless in his search for military success in the Spanish Civil War. Under Chamberlain the British government suggested talks, and indicated that Spain should be put on one side as there were more important issues. At this point Franco sent to Mussolini asking the Italian fleet to strike against Russian ships and any other transports which were bringing help to the Republicans. Mussolini agreed to help, though he refused to use surface ships in such attacks. British, French, Greek and Danish cargo ships were all attacked by 'unknown' submarines. Other neutral ships were attacked because the Fascists believed that they were carrying Russian materials, and because they were not very careful over what ships were sunk.

These attacks roused the British and French. Britain sent four more destroyers to the Mediterranean. The *Havock* had already replied to an attack by dropping depth charges. Interested powers were invited to a naval conference at Nyon in Switzerland. Italy and Germany were absent but Ciano ordered the naval attacks to cease for the moment. The Nyon Conference agreed that France and Britain should patrol the Mediterranean and attack any suspicious submarine or aircraft. Mussolini was furious and promptly sent two submarines to Franco. The 'unknown' submarines had shown their colours. Mussolini then demanded 'parity' of duties with the other powers to patrol the Mediterranean. The British government welcomed the chance for friendly agreement with Italy. The Nyon agreement was changed so that Italy should patrol a zone in the Mediterranean. This meant that she could continue to send supplies to Majorca without being watched. The Italian forces continued to play their part on Franco's side in the war, and did not return home until June 1938. Mussolini's quick victory had not been gained.

10 The Axis Powers

Growing Friendship with Hitler

In order to carry out some of his schemes Hitler required Italian friendship. Hitler did not want a repeat of his failure to gain Austria in 1934. In the summer of 1936 Hitler sent a message to Ciano that Germany would recognize the Italian empire whenever Mussolini wished. Ciano then visited Hitler at Berchtesgaden and the Fuehrer set out to charm his guest. Mussolini was referred to as the leading statesman in the world, and Ciano was soon won over by the warmth of his welcome. He returned home quite dazzled by Hitler. Italy was becoming enmeshed in Spain and Mussolini agreed that Italy and Germany should draw closer together. An agreement was signed and Mussolini mentioned this in a rather jumbled speech at Milan.

'This Berlin–Rome line is not a diaphragm but rather an axis, around which can revolve all those European states with a will to collaboration and peace.' From this speech one phrase was taken and remembered. The 'axis' was to assume a great importance in European affairs.

In 1937 Mussolini went to Libya where he opened a new road along the coast to the Egyptian frontier. He also received the Sword of Islam and made a number of speeches which showed that Italy was Britain's rival in Africa. Then in September 1937 he visited Germany. Hitler met the Duce at Munich and for five days every effort was made to impress Mussolini. The pictures and flowers in Mussolini's rooms were carefully selected. Hitler talked of his teacher who had shown the way for Fascism. He even reminded people that he had once written requesting a signed photograph of Mussolini. The request had been refused then but now Mussolini was charmed by the care taken over his welfare. He was so delighted that he appointed the Fuehrer, 'honorary corporal of the Fascist militia', which was his own rank.

The might of Germany was put on display. The Italians

Hitler and Mussolini, the Fascist partners

watched massive parades. They were taken to see army
manœuvres at Mecklenburg where the latest German guns
were used. Then they were taken to Essen to see these same
guns being made in the Krupp steel foundries. On the evening
of 27 September Mussolini's special train drew near Berlin. He
was tired but deeply impressed by all he had seen. The
Germans were so efficient. Suddenly Hitler's train thundered
alongside Mussolini's. The two mighty engines were aligned
and over the last miles to Berlin they moved at exactly the
same pace to signify 'the parallelism of the two revolutions'.
Just before they reached Berlin Hitler's train spurted ahead so
that he could meet Mussolini when the Italian train arrived.

In Berlin there were banners everywhere. Golden Roman
eagles and Fascist emblems decorated the buildings. The carefully assembled crowds had been brought to Berlin in special
trains and a public holiday had been declared. The S.S. lined
the route and every now and again police dogs with their
handlers could be seen patrolling behind the crowds. Everything had been organized with care and thoroughness. A
tremendous cheer greeted the two leaders and Mussolini stood
up in the open car to acknowledge the crowd. Hitler remained

sitting and even drew back a little so that his guest might receive the full acclaim of the German people.

The next day a huge crowd was assembled in the Olympic stadium. Hitler spoke first and then as the rain poured down Mussolini replied in his clumsy German. He stressed the Fascist belief in loyalty to one's friends and went on to say that from that moment on 115 million souls would become united 'in one single unshakable determination'. The crowd soaked by the rain roared their approval and sang their anthems. They were not much impressed by their new ally. They remembered the 1914–18 War and they considered that Mussolini looked old and tired. On the other hand Mussolini had been deeply impressed by the strength and discipline of the German nation. He returned home from his visit determined to toughen his own regime.

As an early move he decided to introduce the Prussian goose step. He called it the Roman step and pointed out to the outraged Italian King that: 'The goose is a Roman animal—it saved the Capitol.' Also Mussolini finally withdrew from the

Mussolini demonstrates 'the Roman step'

League of Nations late in 1937 to show his support for Germany, who had withdrawn over four years before. The German alliance was actually signed by Mussolini when he agreed to join the Anti-Comintern Pact made between Japan and Germany the previous year. This pact was formed to oppose the Comintern, the Communist International set up in Moscow in 1919 to spread communism throughout the world.

The Austrian Question

Hitler now turned his attention to Austria again. In 1938 the Austrian Chancellor, Schuschnigg, was bullied by Hitler into signing an agreement which virtually meant the end of Austrian independence. The Austrian Nazis were encouraged to demonstrate and Schuschnigg decided to appeal to a popular vote as to whether or not Austria should accept German control. Hitler was not going to wait for a vote which might go against him and German tanks clanked over the Austrian frontier. Hitler was still worried about the possibility of Italian action. He could not afford an open fight which might bring French and British action. He sent Prince Philip of Hesse, who was married to Victor Emmanuel's second daughter and who was a Fascist, as a special messenger to Mussolini. The message began: 'In this fateful hour I turn to you, Excellency, to inform you of a decision which the circumstances have seemed to demand and which cannot now be changed . . .'

The German tanks were moving into Austria to restore order and the German frontier would reach to the Brenner. But, as Ciano wrote of those events:

'The Duce is pleased and tells Hesse to inform the Fuehrer that Italy watches the events with absolute calm.' Hitler was almost delirious with relief, as he had no wish to meet the Italian forces in Austria. He repeated again and again when he heard the news from Prince Philip of Hesse: 'Then please tell Mussolini I will never forget him for this.'

The Italian people were not pleased at the way in which Germany had been allowed to move into Austria. The Anschluss, the German union with Austria, led to a wave of ill-feeling against Mussolini. The Fascist propaganda was strained to the limit and it almost appeared as if Mussolini was losing his grip on affairs. An agreement with Britain signed on 16 April 1938 was rather like a bad joke at this stage, though Ciano regarded it as an indication of Italy's growing importance.

The Return Visit by Hitler

Such matters were put on one side as Mussolini prepared to entertain Hitler. The houses along the line from the Brenner Pass to Naples were whitewashed and decorated with Fascist slogans. Banners and illuminations were arranged and set up in Rome. The Germans took care to send a large number of their own secret police to check the security arrangements although the Italians arrested over 6,000 suspects.

The visit was not as successful from the start as Mussolini's visit to Germany. The Roman crowd was unenthusiastic and,

Mussolini, Hitler, and King Victor Emmanuel watch a parade in Rome, 1938

as a visiting head of state, Hitler had to stay with the King. This he found trying. He disliked the old-fashioned carriage in which he was drawn to the palace, and he disliked the frigid courtesy of the court. Such behaviour Hitler considered out of date and he longed for an open car and the familiar friendliness of the blackshirts. The King was polite and no more. He disliked Hitler and his followers. Soon stories were being spread abroad about the strange way in which Hitler behaved.

The displays and parades went on and, towards the end of his visit, Hitler was impressed by the naval display at Naples. On a perfect day in the lovely setting of the Bay of Naples cruisers and battleships left the harbour in perfect formation. Guns spoke in salute and as a finale submarines surfaced and submerged together all over the bay like a well-schooled shoal of great fish. Hitler's spirits rose. Italy had a powerful navy and he was away from Rome and the dreary King. Then he went to Florence with Mussolini. The Florentine crowds gave him a warm welcome and he was able to drag Mussolini round the main galleries in the city. When Hitler left for Germany Ciano noted that his eyes filled with tears as he said to Mussolini: 'No force can part us any longer.'

German Domination

One of the worst results of these meetings was the way in which Mussolini became increasingly dominated by Hitler. His photographs show that he was ageing fast and he began to lose some of his ability to choose the popular move. He was even prepared to admit that he ran a political risk by installing Clara Petacci as his permanent mistress in 1936. More and more Mussolini began to drift and he allowed his policy to become dominated by German thought and German plans. He decided to adopt the German racial theories. There were about 47,000 Jews in Italy, and there was virtually no anti-Semitism. In July 1938 a manifesto drawn up by Mussolini and a group of professors was published. It stated that there was a pure Italian race and that the Jews did not belong to it. Decrees were issued forbidding the entry of foreign Jews into Italian schools and then forbidding foreign Jews to settle in

Clara Petacci

Italy or her dominions. Jews who had fled from Germany and
Austria had to move on once more. Under later decrees
Italians were forbidden to marry Jews and Italian Jews were
forbidden to join the Fascist party or the army. The Italians
were not interested in these moves and the only real persecu-
tion of Italian Jews came when the Germans held the north of
Italy during the war. The Fascist propaganda machine failed
to rouse enthusiasm for the race theory. Mussolini was beginning to lose control of the situation in his effort to keep up with
Hitler.

Munich

The flickering flame of Mussolini's popular appeal was kindled
for an instant by his action at Munich in 1938. For a moment
he appeared to have broken free from German domination
and once more he heard the enthusiastic cheers of the Italian
people. Now that he had gained Austria Hitler turned his
attention to Czechoslovakia. He was determined to use the $3\frac{1}{4}$
million who made up the German minority in the Sudeten

areas as his excuse for moving into Czechoslovakia. These Germans had been subjects of the Austrian Empire before 1919 and Hitler carefully fostered their German feelings. President Beneš of Czechoslovakia took a firm line with Sudeten German unrest. In May 1938 Hitler's plans received a setback. Beneš prepared to mobilize in the face of German troop movements and he appealed to the powers for help. Hitler saw that the Germans were unwilling to go to war at this point so he prepared to wait for the time being. During this period the Germans refused to give the Italian government any idea of their plans. Rumour ran wild in Rome. By September 1938 it became obvious that Hitler intended to take over the Sudetenland from Czechoslovakia. Chamberlain, the British prime minister, made desperate efforts to keep peace. Mussolini merely said: 'As soon as Hitler sees that old man, he will know that he has won the battle.' Mussolini felt that if Hitler was out to revenge Versailles it would be better to be on the side of the German military machine. He pledged his support to Germany.

Germany prepared her armies and there was general mobilization in Czechoslovakia. The British fleet began to concentrate and the French army was on the move. Europe was on the brink of war in September 1938. Mussolini remained calm and it is difficult to know whether or not he would in fact have marched with the Germans at this time. However, on 28 September, Chamberlain, who was in despair, appealed to Mussolini to save Europe from the catastrophe of war. Mussolini agreed to do what he could. He telephoned Attolico, his ambassador in Berlin, and told him to see Hitler. Attolico was to tell Hitler that Mussolini pledged his support and then suggest a delay of twenty-four hours before mobilization. Hatless Attolico ran on his desperate errand. Hitler was in discussion with the French ambassador when he received Attolico's panted message. He thought for a moment and then agreed to pause for further negotiation. A conference between Britain, France, Italy and Germany was suggested and Mussolini chose Munich as the meeting place. Chamberlain was filled with relief and he left for Munich at once. Daladier for France also agreed to attend. Mussolini was delighted. He considered Britain's weakness in the face of German force to be

an obvious sign of decadence. Hitler arranged to meet
Mussolini on the way to Munich. He unrolled his maps and
explained his plans as if his armies were already on the move.
Mussolini was silent. In the end he turned to Hitler and asked

Munich Conference, 1938. Front row from left, Neville Chamberlain, Daladier,
Hitler, Mussolini, Ciano

him what he would accept without war. He was handed the
German demands and these formed the basis of the eventual
agreement.

At the meeting everything was ill prepared and Mussolini
appeared very much in control. Hitler remained tense and
silent while Mussolini genially talked to Daladier in French
and to Chamberlain in adequate English. The discussions
went on and the powers agreed that Germany should have the
Sudetenland under various conditions. The agreement was
signed when ink had been found for the inkstand early on the
morning of 30 September. The next day German troops

marched into the Sudetenland and it became obvious that the conditions were going to be forgotten. President Beneš went into exile and Czechoslovakia was virtually destroyed. Hitler had gained the Sudetenland without war and Germany was delighted. The Germans began to forget how near war the Fuehrer's policy had brought them. Churchill stated firmly to the House of Commons: 'We are in the presence of a disaster of the first magnitude.' Mussolini returned home to a hero's welcome. He had saved Europe from war and the Italian people rejoiced. Mussolini himself was not content for he felt that such demonstrations showed a lack of the true aggressive spirit of the Fascist.

11   The Outbreak of War

'Give the Germans a great deal of sausage, butter, beer and a cheap car, and they will never want to risk their skins.'
[Mussolini in 1939]

The German War

Hitler had no intention of halting his plans for further negotiation. In March 1939 the Germans occupied the whole of Czechoslovakia. This action persuaded Mussolini that the Italians must show similar Fascist determination. The anti-German feeling in Italy was growing and Mussolini had to act at once if he was to prove his ability to carry out an equally swift and successful campaign. King Zog of Albania was presented with an ultimatum. Albania was already under Italian influence for Zog relied on Italian support and had allowed the Italians to control Albanian oil. However, complete control of Albania would give the Italians a hold over the entrance to the Adriatic and Ciano had always encouraged the idea of an Albanian invasion.

Forces, including four Bersaglieri regiments and an infantry division, were prepared in southern Italy. The capture of Madrid by Franco's forces convinced Mussolini that he could afford to act. On Good Friday 1939 the Italians attacked Albania. The military operation was not a success. It was said that a competent fire brigade could have swept the Italians back into the sea. King Zog had no such competent force. He decided to flee with his wife, who was expecting a baby, and his family to Greece. The Albanians looted the capital city of Tirana until armed volunteers restored order. The Italian army then appeared on the scene and Mussolini claimed that Albania had been brought under Italian control. No preparations had been made for the administration of the new dominion and it was a rather hollow victory. Britain and France regarded the affair with sad indifference, for they were concentrating on the next German move.

Clash of interests in the Balkans

Goering attended the ceremony in Rome when the Albanian crown was presented to Victor Emmanuel. Mussolini was most struck by the aggressive talk of his German guest. He tried to impress Goering by ordering the anti-aircraft defence round Rome to be brought into action. Unfortunately the Italians had to bring in field artillery to make any real show at all. Mussolini insisted that the Axis needed three years of peace to prepare for war. Albania had shown the Italians that the legions of bayonets were far from ready. Ribbentrop agreed that three years would be useful time for preparation and

75

drew up an alliance which would shackle Italy to the German
war machine. In May 1939 the two foreign ministers, Ciano
for Italy and Ribbentrop for Germany, signed a treaty in
Berlin. Mussolini soon named the treaty, the Pact of Steel.

Mussolini was convinced that Germany was preparing for a
period of peaceful consolidation and in any event he wished to
be on the side of such a power. His rear would be safe if he

The Italian Empire, 1939

turned his attention to making the Mediterranean an Italian lake. Hitler had no intention of consulting Mussolini and he was already planning his attack on Poland. The Germans showed this determination to go ahead without consulting the Italians again and again. Ciano returned from a meeting at Salzburg convinced that Italy and Germany could not work together. Mussolini remained uncertain and felt that he could trust Hitler.

In August 1939 Hitler negotiated a pact with Russia. The Italians were not consulted and the stage was set for the attack on Poland by the German forces. Hitler was convinced that Britain and France would give way again but he felt that the Axis should make a show of unity and strength. On 25 August Hitler wrote to Mussolini explaining his moves against Poland. Mussolini replied that his country was not prepared for war. Hitler hesitated. He also heard that Britain had just signed a mutual assistance pact with Poland. He wrote again to Mussolini asking what supplies Italy needed to put her on a war footing. Mussolini was persuaded to send a massive list of requirements to show how unwilling Italy was to go to war. The list included demands for 10,000 tons of lead and 150 anti-aircraft batteries with ammunition. Mussolini made a plea for peace or at least negotiation. At the same time he pointed out that the Fuehrer had his loyal support. Hitler decided that he would have to move without Italian military support. He was determined to attack Poland and he had no intention of halting his army again.

Mussolini could only watch helplessly. He could not afford to act and he had no clear idea of what he should do. His only chance would be another Munich. When Britain cut her communications with Rome Mussolini was quick to assure the British ambassador that Italy would not enter the war. The next day the German troops invaded Poland. Italy remained neutral. On 3 September Britain and France declared war on Germany and the Second World War had begun. Mussolini, the great Fascist warrior, was unwillingly on the sidelines for the next nine months. Hitler was, for once, very patient. He worked quietly to bring his friend and ally into the war. He used the Italian train as the place for their discussion as a mark of respect when the two leaders met at the Brenner Pass

Hitler dominates the Axis partnership, 1940

in March 1940. Mussolini became more and more convinced that Germany would win the war and that Italy must act quickly if she was to gain prestige and territory.

The Parallel War

Mussolini believed that Italy must prove her greatness as a military power. He had begun to believe his own propaganda about the power of the Italian war machine. His theory was that Italy should fight a parallel war. The Germans would act in northern Europe while the Italians made the Mediterranean their own. The 'prison bars' in the Mediterranean and the 'sentinels' of Gibraltar and the Suez Canal would be broken and captured by the defeat of Britain and France. The Axis alliance was Mussolini's answer to the obvious opposition which Britain and France would show to his Mediterranean schemes. At least he argued that this was so in his outline of policy to the Fascist Grand Council. Furthermore he argued that his northern frontier would be safe under an alliance with Germany.

Such arguments could be used to support the idea of a war fought alongside Germany in Italian interests. The danger lay in the fact that the Italians would find themselves fighting a war in German interests. Mussolini was aware of this danger. The invasion of Albania was to show the Germans that Italy had her own interests. At the same time Mussolini was in a cruel position. He admired the efficiency of the Hitler regime and he was determined to gain something from the German success. As he watched the German armies sweep over Europe Mussolini became convinced that he must take the gamble of starting the parallel war. Also it was difficult for a man who had spent so many years claiming that Fascists were tough and relentless to stand back and watch other nations fight. He decided that Italy must fight alongside Germany. This was a sad mistake for not only did Hitler dominate Mussolini but also the Italian forces were used as expendable pawns by the Germans. The fortunes of Italy under her Fascist regime became linked with the fortunes of Hitler's regime.

The success of the German invasion of Norway and Denmark, undertaken with no word to Italy, seemed to prove German power. The success of the German invasion of Holland and Belgium on 10 May 1940 convinced many Italians that Mussolini was right to plan to take part in the war. Churchill, who had become prime minister of Britain on the same day as the Germans launched their attack on Holland and Belgium, made one last appeal to the Duce: 'Is it too late to stop a river of blood from flowing between the British and Italian peoples?'

It was too late. Mussolini's desire for action was fanned by the steady stream of progress reports which Hitler sent him. Mussolini boasted of his military preparations and on 10 June 1940 the British and French ambassadors were told that Italy declared war. The French ambassador turned to Ciano and said in parting: 'The Germans are hard masters. You too will learn this.'

That evening Mussolini announced his decision from his balcony:

'We are entering the lists against the plutocratic and reactionary democracies of the West . . .'

There was very little enthusiasm for Mussolini's war in

Italy. Gloom seemed to settle over Rome after the announcement and Ciano felt that it was a sad day for Italy. Mussolini took on the office of Minister of War and became commander-in-chief of the armed forces instead of the King. So certain was he that victory was in sight that he linked himself completely to the war fought alongside his German ally.

12   The Anvil of War

'No one has ever cast a doubt on the bravery of the Italian soldier. Should a doubt exist, let him visit Italian battle-fields and the last remnants of his scepticism will be shamed out of his heart.'

Lloyd George, *Memoirs*

Italian Military Weakness 1940

Hitler was happy that Mussolini should join him in the war, though the German generals were less enthusiastic. There was no joint military co-ordination between the two powers and Hitler continued to inform Mussolini of his schemes after he had set them going. Still Hitler believed that Mussolini might prove a useful ally. He had been impressed by the Italian fleet and he had listened to Mussolini's statement that seventy Italian divisions were ready to march. Mussolini often boasted that he could mobilize 'eight million bayonets'.

The manpower for such a force did just exist and the Italians could be brave soldiers. Lloyd George wrote in his *Memoirs* about the bravery of the Italians on the Austrian front in the First World War. *Crusader*, the Eighth Army's weekly paper, mentioned that the Folgore division in the battle of El Alamein showed itself, 'the equal in discipline and fighting qualities of the German 90th Light'. During the war the Savoy Grenadiers, the Bersaglieri, Italian airmen, and the crews of one-man submarines all fought with distinction on various occasions. However, the majority of the Italian forces were not interested in Mussolini's war. Fascist propaganda failed to move them. Their songs were not of the glory of war but of its futility. Two verses from one of the more cheerful songs in the official army song book show this.

> Captain, captain of the guard
> Summon the buglers all,
> Make them stand in the barrack square
> And sound the demob call.

> Driver, driver of the train
> Start your engine off.
> We're in a hurry to get home,
> Of war we've had enough.

Many Italian reserve officers were unenthusiastic about the war and some of the generals were Fascist politicians rather than soldiers. Mussolini should have studied the morale of his armed forces and taken the advice given in the Italian cavalry manual: 'Before approaching the horse, look at its face and study its expression. If this is not reassuring, put yourself on guard.'

The Italians lacked the desire to fight and this feeling was strengthened by their poor equipment. Fascist propaganda was no substitute for ammunition and bayonets. The Italian infantry complained that the Albanian campaign proved that their boots had soles of cardboard. In 1940 the Italians had two searchlights and 230 anti-aircraft batteries for the air defence of their country. Artillery in 1940 was largely made up of old equipment used in 1918 which included some old Austrian guns. Trucks were in desperately short supply, about 42,000 vehicles in all, and when parades had been ordered in the period before the war the police had lent their lorries painted khaki for the occasion. In Libya this shortage of transport was one of the reasons for the large number of Italians taken prisoner. They were unable to withdraw over the desert like the British and the Germans because they did not have the transport. Tanks were also in short supply. The armoured divisions in Libya were supposed to contain five tank battalions of fifty-two tanks each. In fact they contained three such tank battalions at the most. The number of Italian aircraft ready for action was said to be over 3,000 in 1939. Ciano learnt from the jealous naval authorities that the number was only 982. When a census was taken planes were flown from one station to another to give a false appearance of strength.

The Italian navy which had so impressed Hitler was without any naval air arm at all. This weakness was to lead to disaster in November 1940 just at the time when Mussolini had persuaded the Germans to allow Italian planes to take part in the air attack on Britain. Winston Churchill described the destruction of the power of the Italian fleet in his *Second World War*:

'Taranto lies in the heel of Italy three hundred and twenty miles from Malta. Its magnificent harbour was heavily defended against all modern forms of attack. The arrival at Malta of some fast reconnaissance machines enabled us to discern our prey. The British plan was to fly two waves of aircraft from the *Illustrious*, the first of twelve and the second of nine, of which eleven were to carry torpedoes, and the rest either bombs or flares. The *Illustrious* released her aircraft shortly after dark from a point about a hundred and seventy miles from Taranto. For an hour the battle raged amid fire and destruction among the Italian ships. Despite the heavy flak only two of our aircraft were shot down. The rest flew safely back to the *Illustrious*.

'By this single stroke the balance of naval power in the Mediterranean was decisively altered.'

Half the Italian fleet was disabled for at least six months because the Italians were not provided with any fleet air arm.

On land the Italian forces had really fared little better than the Italian navy. The invasion of the Riviera had not been a success. The attack upon France was launched after the French had asked the Germans for an armistice. The Italian forces were not prepared for an offensive and divisions became snarled up in the Alpine foothills while they hastily deployed. The frontier towns of Modane and Briançon were taken and then the Italian attack was halted in the streets of Mentone. Mussolini had to go to the peace talks virtually empty-handed.

The Germans were courteous but were interested in gaining the friendship of the French Vichy government. They were particularly keen that the French fleet should not go over to Britain. Mussolini was not going to be allowed to take vast areas of French territory and he only held a few acres by force. He was made to take second place at the peace discussions and, after the Franco-German armistice had been signed at Compiègne on 22 June 1940, Mussolini quietly signed an armistice with the French at the Villa Ineisa near Rome. Italy only gained the small frontier area she had taken in her initial attack.

Britain now stood alone and Mussolini feared that she would come to terms with Germany before he could gain anything. He feared that he would be too late as he had been in his attack on France. He forgot that Italy was not ready for a major war. The Battle of Britain was well under way when Mussolini forced his unwilling commander in Libya to attack Egypt. On 13 September 1940 the Italian main army moved across the Egyptian frontier while other forces probed into the Sudan and Kenya. Within three days the Italians had ad-

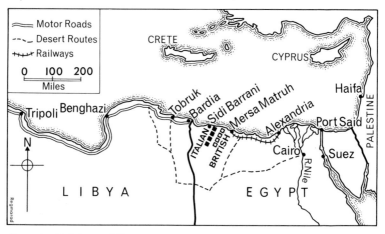

Campaign in Libya and Egypt, 1940

vanced sixty miles to Sidi Barrani. They were to stay there for the next three months. The British had made a planned fighting withdrawal in the face of the enormous Italian numbers.

Mussolini was delighted. Hitler was less happy. Franco would not join the war even for the bait of Gibraltar, and Vichy France could not be persuaded to attack Britain. At the same time the Soviet Union was demanding Bessarabia from Rumania. There was increasing hostility between Berlin and Moscow, and this centred on the important oil wells and the grain of Rumania. Hitler decided to move German troops into Rumania, supposedly to protect the Rumanian government.

Mussolini was furious at this action. He regarded the Balkans as an Italian area in the parallel war. As a result he decided to show Hitler that Italy could play her full part in the war. The Italians could occupy Greece and Hitler would not be told of the plan. Mussolini delayed his message to the Fuehrer until his army was ready to move late in October 1940. Hitler tried to stop the attack and arranged to meet Mussolini in Florence on 28 October. When he arrived he was greeted by Mussolini and told: 'Victorious Italian troops crossed the Greco-Albanian frontier at dawn today.' Hitler accepted the move quite cheerfully and Mussolini felt that all was well.

Italian attack on Greece, 1940

Within a few days disaster had overcome all Mussolini's plans. He learnt that the attack on Greece had been repulsed and that the Greeks were on the offensive. He also learnt of the loss of part of his fleet at Taranto and of the British occupation of Crete. Early in December 1940 a desperate Mussolini had to send to Hitler for help in order to save the Italian forces in Greece. On 9 December the British launched a counter-attack on Sidi Barrani. Within a month the British army was to advance 200 miles and take 113,000 Italian prisoners. The situation was gloomy. The hope of a quick victory was lost and the Germans ceased to talk of the parallel war. Hitler agreed to send help but he refused to send more raw materials. The Germans began to move into Italy with supplies of equipment. German economic experts were everywhere in Italy and some Germans considered that Italy should be taken over as Rumania had been. Mussolini's Fascist bluster had led him into a war in which Italy became a German vassal state.

The End of the Italian Empire, 1941

1941 was to prove a year of disasters for the Italians. General Wavell, the British commander in the Middle East, had a force of about 90,000 troops with which to protect British interests. The Italians had forces of over 400,000, and in face of this superior force Wavell had pulled in his front and abandoned British Somaliland. In September 1940 a force of fifty heavy tanks had reached Wavell. Churchill had decided to risk sending these precious tanks to the Middle East even though Britain faced the threat of invasion. The action proved to be the right one for Wavell was able to launch a raid against the Italians late in 1940. This met with such success that it was turned into an all-out offensive. Bardia fell on 5 February and Tobruk soon after. A tank force crossed the desert and cut the coast road from Benghazi. The Italian forces in Libya were routed. They had been defeated by a much smaller force which moved swiftly and aggressively.

The British then launched further attacks on the Italian possessions. Eritrea was invaded from the Sudan and after stiff fighting at Keren it was cleared of Italians by April 1941. Abyssinia was invaded from Kenya and on 4 April 1941 the Emperor Haile Selassie was restored to his throne after nearly five years of exile. From north and south the British forces converged on Amba Alagi and in May 1941 Italian East Africa was in British hands. Once again the Italians had shown little desire to fight for their empire and the Duce, while the British had been helped by Abyssinian guerrillas.

Wavell's advance in Libya was halted so that help could be sent to the Greeks. The Italian attack had been held and pushed back by the Greek forces but it was obvious that the Germans intended to intervene. Hitler was planning his Russian offensive and he had to have the Balkans under his control. The Yugoslav government accepted German domination and were then overthrown in the name of the youthful King Peter. The Germans then attacked in April 1941. At the same time German forces moved into Greece. Within two weeks the Germans had conquered and the British were being evacuated from Greece. On 20 May the Germans made a massive airborne attack on Crete and by the end of the month they had taken the island. Yet the Italians had met with no real successes and their fleet, badly mauled at Taranto, was again hit hard at the battle of Matapan. The Italian heavy cruiser *Pola* was sunk along with two other cruisers and several destroyers at no cost to the British fleet under the command of Admiral Cunningham.

Even in North Africa the Germans took control. On 31 March Rommel attacked the British front. By the middle of May his tanks were at the Egyptian frontier and only Tobruk held out behind his victorious counterattack. Mussolini was particularly upset by Rommel's victory. He ordered Graziani, the Italian commander, to face a court of inquiry and he sadly pointed out that troops could not be led by a man who remained 'seventy feet underground in a Roman tomb'. Graziani's feelings were significant and showed up the feeling of the Italian army for as he said to his wife, 'you cannot break armour with finger-nails alone'. Mussolini felt that his armies had failed him, and at the same time his efforts at diplomacy were futile. Hitler told him nothing. They met in January 1941 at Berchtesgaden and Hitler pointed out that he considered a German invasion of Greece to be necessary. He also persuaded Mussolini to approach Franco. This Mussolini did at Bordighera. He met with no success. In addition Mussolini annoyed party leaders by ordering them to the front. In the snows of the Albanian front Fascist leaders began to question the leadership of Mussolini.

Mussolini's complete dependence on the Germans was proved in the summer of 1941. In May he was summoned to the Brenner for a meeting. Hitler held forth once again about his determination to destroy Britain and did not give any indication that his plans for attacking Russia were complete. The troop concentrations indicated such action and Mussolini was not surprised when he was dragged out of bed on the morning of 22 June to be told that the Germans had invaded Russia. There was only one thing that he could do and that was to join in so that he could share the German success. He believed victory was around the corner and the Italians must be in at the kill. Troops were hastily assembled and sent to the Russian front. Pleased by the success of the early stages of the campaign Hitler invited Mussolini to visit his headquarters in the forests at Rastenburg. The two leaders toured the front and Mussolini felt that Hitler treated him without real respect because he went off and chatted to the troops. He felt better when he piloted their aeroplane back from the front, much to Hitler's dismay. Mussolini tried to persuade Hitler to announce the 'European New Order' as an answer to the Atlantic Charter. This idea was that Bolshevism should be wiped out and that there should be peaceful co-operation amongst European nations. Hitler was prepared to use the idea as propaganda but he intended to dominate Europe. Mussolini returned from the Russian front feeling depressed. It was obvious that Italy was now involved in a German war and that her only hope was a quick victory. This hope grew dimmer and dimmer in 1941. Early in December the German advance in Russia halted short of Moscow and the Japanese attacked Pearl Harbor. Mussolini was pleased and calmly agreed to join Japan although Italy was only bound by treaty to do so if Japan was attacked. In a short speech from the balcony of the Palazzo Venezia the Duce announced that Italy declared war on the United States on 11 December. The short, victorious campaign had now become an extended war and Mussolini could only hope that a smashing German victory would save him. The Italian people only wanted peace.

The Turning Point, 1942

1942 began gloomily for the Italians. They were tired of the war and they were short of food. The British navy were sinking many Italian supply ships and the Germans were not sending much material for replacement. In addition the Germans in Italy behaved more like conquerors than allies, while Italians

Mussolini trying to encourage the Italian people

labouring in Germany were treated badly. Mussolini made a tour of Italy early in 1942 in an effort to arouse enthusiasm for the war. The audiences cheered him, but he sensed that he was losing touch with the masses. Goering's visit to Rome did not make feelings any warmer between the Germans and the Italians. Ciano found Goering arrogant and bloated and prepared to talk about little except his jewels. Hitler learnt of this lack of enthusiasm and again summoned Mussolini to listen to a talk on the state of the Axis. The one military operation discussed at this Salzburg conference was an attack on Malta.

D

Malta was the base from which the British operated against the Axis supply line to Africa, and their operations were proving successful. In November 1941 Rommel had been driven back because he was short of supplies. The British forces relieved Tobruk on 9 December 1941. As a result of this defeat the Axis powers were forced to turn their attention to the problem of supply for their African forces. The British fleet received a series of heavy blows late in 1941. On 12 November the *Ark Royal* was torpedoed after flying aircraft into Malta. On 18 December an Italian submarine sent three 'human torpedoes' into Alexandria harbour. Time bombs were set which seriously damaged the battleships *Queen Elizabeth* and *Valiant*. Other ships were badly damaged or sunk in a minefield when trying to intercept an Italian convoy. Malta was forced to fight for its life as the Germans moved a whole air corps from Russia to Sicily and North Africa. Mussolini wished to take Malta, and airborne troops were trained for operation 'Hercules', which would take place in July 1942.

Rommel was receiving supplies early in 1942 as a result of the effort to neutralize the British hold on the Mediterranean. His counterattack was so successful that the scheme to attack Malta was shelved. Both Hitler and Rommel saw the prospect of triumph in Egypt as the British forces were rolled back. In June 1942 the advance was within sixty-five miles of Alexandria. Hitler wrote to Mussolini: 'Order operations to be continued until the British forces are completely annihilated. The goddess of fortune passes only once close to warriors in battle. Anyone who does not grasp her at that moment can very often never touch her again.'

Mussolini could not resist the chance for glory in Egypt, so the attack on Malta was postponed and Mussolini flew out to join his troops. He saw himself leading the victory parade through Cairo and holding aloft the Sword of Islam. He arrived just as Rommel had been halted at Alamein. For three weeks Mussolini hung about behind the battle line and inspected troops and hospitals. Rommel never bothered to visit him and the desert veterans regarded him with amusement. In disgust he returned home a sick and broken man.

Mussolini now sank into a state of grim suffering. He was the victim of a complete nervous collapse. Bottai wrote of him at this time: 'The man seems not so much ill as humiliated, sad and unable to struggle against his advancing years.' Mussolini and the Italian people waited for the next blow. The Italian convoys were under pressure from Malta again, and in October Montgomery launched his attack against the Axis forces at Alamein. Rommel was in Berlin when the attack started and when he returned he ordered a counterattack. The battle raged between the tank forces and by 4 November

North Africa and Italy 1942–43

the Axis forces had to retreat. On 8 November American and British forces landed in French North Africa, at Casablanca, Oran and Algiers. Hitler occupied the rest of France, while the French scuttled their fleet at Toulon to keep it out of Axis hands. The Germans also poured troops into Tunis instead of drawing in their front. Mussolini encouraged such action for prestige reasons as he regarded Africa as an Italian front. Nobody could hide the fact that the war was going badly and the Vatican tried to have Rome declared an open city. Mussolini had foreseen a short and glorious war which would increase his hold over Italy. Now he began to pay the price for his mistake.

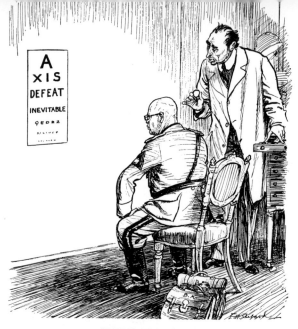

READING WITH TEARS

"Give me some pinker ones. I can still read it."

[Signor Mussolini, it is reported, has been advised to wear spectacles.]

'Reading with Tears'

Invasion, 1943

The Germans were heavily involved against Russia and Mussolini began to feel that the only hope for Italy lay in making peace with Russia. If both Germany and Italy made such a peace it would be possible for the Axis to concentrate on the area of the Mediterranean and so gain victory. At Salzburg in April 1943 Mussolini put this scheme to Hitler. He received no encouragement and the divergent aims of the two Axis powers became clearer than ever. The Italians wished to end the war whereas Hitler was determined to carry on and smash Russia.

In Rome Mussolini's failure to make any impression on Hitler's plans was viewed with alarm. Anfuso wrote: 'After two decades of Fascism, Rome was plotting.' Mussolini spoke from his balcony but failed to rouse the crowd to any show of enthusiasm for war. Words were no longer enough. The whole Fascist image had been shattered by military defeat. The Germans viewed matters in Italy with cold realism. They made military plans to take over Italy while Mussolini fell ill again. The King was approached by politicians and military leaders. He was determined to find a constitutional solution and he was afraid that if Mussolini was dismissed the Germans would move in. He felt that Mussolini was preferable to Hitler, so he acted cautiously.

While the Italians plotted in Rome the Allies prepared the invasion of Sicily. The Axis forces in Africa had surrendered on 12 May 1943. British, Canadian and American troops were organized for the invasion of Sicily which took place on the night of 9 July. The only serious resistance came from the German troops in Sicily and they managed to delay the advance for five weeks before they withdrew to the mainland. The Italians put up token resistance only. The invaders found pictures of Mussolini riddled with bullets and houses painted with welcoming slogans like, '*Viva il Colonello Stevens*'. Colonel Stevens was the B.B.C. broadcaster on the Italian wavelength. The Italians were sick of the war, and now fighting was taking place on Italian soil. Against this background Mussolini's political fall took place.

A picture of Mussolini 'riddled with bullets'

13 The End of the Duce

Political Defeat, 1943

The military situation was desperate and Mussolini agreed to call a meeting of the Fascist Grand Council. Before this meeting could take place he agreed to meet Hitler at Feltre. Mussolini would have to persuade Hitler to allow Italy to make peace if he hoped to survive as the Duce. Under such desperate circumstances Mussolini seemed to lack the will to plan the meeting and he shut himself away from any advisers. The meeting at Feltre took place on 19 July 1943, and Hitler delivered his usual talk on the state of affairs. Mussolini, tired and ill, sat listening. Hitler attacked the Italian war effort and Mussolini continued to sit silent and uncomfortable.

During the meeting a message was brought to the two leaders. It told them that Rome was under heavy air attack. This news upset the Italians present and Mussolini himself was deeply shaken. Hitler with no regard for their feelings continued his monologue. The meeting ended without any satisfactory conclusion. In parting Mussolini said to Hitler: 'Ours is a common cause, Fuehrer.' To his followers Mussolini merely pointed out that the Germans had promised faithfully to send help and military supplies.

The Italians returned gloomily to Rome. Many were now determined that Mussolini must go because he was unable to break free from Germany and make peace. The King warned Mussolini that Italy could not carry on much longer, while Grandi openly canvassed support for a motion which would allow the Grand Council to revive the old forms of government.

By 24 July matters had reached a head. A group of generals were planning Mussolini's arrest. Grandi's motion before the Grand Council would give the King a constitutional chance to call on Marshal Badoglio to form a government. In this tense situation the Fascist Grand Council met at five in the afternoon. The members gathered wearing their black shirts and full of nervous uncertainty. Grandi carried two hand grenades and prepared for a dramatic end.

In fact the meeting went off quietly. Mussolini spoke for nearly two hours and made a rambling defence of his actions. There was a short silence when he finished and then two more speakers made muddled speeches before Grandi rose to propose his motion. He proposed that the machinery of government should be restored and Mussolini's control over policy removed. Also he proposed that the King should take back the command of the army from Mussolini. He launched a savage attack on the Duce for taking part in a German war and destroying the Fascist revolution. After this bitter speech the debate continued with a short break during which Mussolini retired. The members of the Council waited uneasily for their arrest by the Fascist militia while Mussolini sat sipping a glass of milk and spooning sugar into his mouth in the next room. He remained passive and unmoved by entreaties that he should arrest the Grand Council and call out the militia. He seemed to be utterly resigned to events and to be thinking more about the pain from his ulcer than political action.

At length Grandi's motion was put to the vote. Nineteen members of the Fascist Grand Council voted in favour of it, seven voted against and three, including Mussolini, did not vote. The harsh fact that Italy could not continue the war had led to Mussolini's defeat by the leaders of his own party.

The next day Mussolini had an audience with the King. Before going to the meeting he refused to agree with Galbiati, commander of the Fascist militia, who argued that the nineteen opposition members of the Grand Council should be arrested at once. Mussolini stated that he would discuss the matter with the King before taking action. At the palace on the other hand plans to arrest Mussolini were put into action. An ambulance followed by a lorry containing a detachment of *carabinieri* drove up to the palace. The Queen had persuaded the King that the Prime Minister should not be arrested within the palace walls so the *carabinieri* took up their positions in the gardens outside. Mussolini was unaware of these hectic arrangements. He convinced himself that he could weather this political storm as he had weathered the troubles in 1924. Mussolini arrived at the palace and was met by the King.

They moved into the audience chamber where the King told Mussolini that the country was in a desperate state. In some excitement he went on to say that he must demand Mussolini's resignation and that he had asked Badoglio to form a government.

Meanwhile Mussolini's chauffeur had been lured into the porter's lodge to answer the telephone. He was held there while the ambulance was backed up to the door. Two *carabinieri* officers waited and met Mussolini as he left the palace. They persuaded him that they had been sent for his protection and then they all climbed into the back of the ambulance. The ambulance shot off down the hot streets taking the Duce to the police barracks at Trastevere. Later he was moved to the police cadet barracks and settled down for the night. As Mussolini saw the sentries outside his door he began to wonder for the first time if he was being protected or arrested.

While Mussolini was in the barracks under guard the Fascist government quietly collapsed. The whole system depended on Mussolini and without him nobody was certain how they should act. Since 1943 the secretary of the party had been Scorza. He was not sure what was happening and in the end he went to the headquarters of the military police for information. He was promptly arrested and only set free on condition that he gave orders to stop the Fascists from action. Scorza went straight into hiding but his staff sent out telegrams to all the party secretaries telling them not to resist the change of government.

Galbiati waited at his headquarters uncertain whether or not he should call out the Fascist militia. He was also in doubt because he had received no orders from the Duce. While he tried to locate his leader the army moved into Rome. Telephone lines were cut so Galbiati was unable to summon his reserve 'M' division. There were only a few scattered units of the Fascist militia at hand in Rome and there was little Galbiati could do as tanks rumbled into the square in front of his headquarters. Quietly he resigned his post and civil war had been avoided.

While all this had been taking place Badoglio had been playing bridge. He now came forward to take over from his military supporters. Three radio messages were sent out to the waiting nation. It was announced that the King accepted Mussolini's resignation and that Badoglio had been appointed in his place. It was also announced that the King would take command of the armed forces and that the war was to continue.

Italian military leaders feared German intervention at this point. Neither Badoglio's government nor the King dared go further though negotiations with the British and the Americans were begun at once. The Germans had already prepared a military plan for taking over Italy in the event of a collapse. They had four divisions fighting in Sicily as well as two armoured divisions in southern Italy. However they only had one division in Sardinia, one motorized division and some parachute groups in central Italy which could have acted on 24 July. The Germans did not hesitate to move up more troops as the situation in Italy became clearer. The German government encouraged Fascist plots while the generals moved seven new divisions into Italy by the end of August. Rommel favoured cautious movement to avoid a direct clash with the Italian army. Badoglio did his best to assure the Germans that Italy would continue to fight while at the same moment he negotiated with the Allies for peace. The situation was tense as the Italian government argued over terms and German troops poured over the Alpine passes into Italy.

The Allies were not prepared to wait too long and on 12 August they bombed Milan and Turin to show that they meant business. On 17 August German and Italian troops were withdrawn from Sicily. Invasion of the Italian mainland was expected and the German commander, Rommel, set up his headquarters for the defence of Italy. Rumour ran wild in Rome and there were Fascist plots to take back control of the government. The King and Badoglio signed surrender terms on 3 September. These were to be announced over the radio by Badoglio on 8 September. On 7 September the German High Command issued orders for the disarming of all Italian units just as the news of the Allied invasion of Italy came through. Allied landings had taken place in Calabria on 3 September and in Salerno a few days later. The Allies had hoped to cut off troops in the southern part of Italy and overrun the mainland. They found stiff German opposition and

Allied troops landing at Salerno, 1943

had to fight every inch of the way up Italy. The Germans regarded Badoglio as a traitor and, when the news of the Italian surrender, which was heard in Berlin by way of a London broadcast, was confirmed, they acted firmly. The Alpine passes were already in their hands and they were able to cut off Italian troops in the Balkans. German troops moved into Rome and destroyed any Italian units who were prepared to fight. The King and Badoglio fled from Rome and by 11 September the Germans were able to declare that Italy was a theatre of war under their military control.

Hitler's early political plans of a counterstroke by Italian Fascists had been shelved while events took this military course. Now that the German army was in control of most of the Italian mainland Hitler returned to his political schemes. He was very keen to demonstrate that the Fascists in Italy had been betrayed and that they could easily revive. Hitler did not want any Germans to look for an example of Fascism in action in Italy at this time. Hitler knew that a puppet Fascist state in Italy must have a leader and he was determined that the leader should be his old friend Mussolini.

Rescue

Mussolini had been moved from place to place by his guards who feared that he would be taken by the Allies or by the

Germans. Badoglio had offered Mussolini a choice of retreat but, when Mussolini asked to go back to Romagna, this was considered too unsafe. The new Council of Ministers sent him to the island of Ponza off Naples. There he celebrated his sixtieth birthday. One cable of greeting was delivered to Mussolini. It had been sent by Goering. Mussolini was then moved to La Maddalena off Sardinia. A German plane flew low over the island, so Mussolini was hurriedly moved to the skiing resort on the slopes of the highest mountain on the Apennines, Gran Sasso. First he stayed in a villa and was then moved up the funicular to a winter-sports hotel at about 7,000 feet. From this lofty prison he was to be rescued by a daring German expedition.

As soon as Hitler was certain that Mussolini was in prison he ordered a special operation to find then release his friend and fellow Fascist dictator. There has been a great deal of argument as to whether the S.S. under Colonel Otto Skorzeny or the paratroops of General Student's command played a greater part in the rescue of Mussolini. In fact the operation seems to have been a success in spite of the rather confused rivalry between various German formations. After a period of careful search in which the Italians managed to keep one step ahead of the Germans, Skorzeny located Mussolini in his prison on the island of Maddalena. Skorzeny himself flew over the island. On the return flight the plane crashed into the sea and the occupants had to be rescued by an E-boat. Before an operation could be launched to land a rescue party on the island Mussolini was moved and the Germans lost the scent again. Once again the Germans tracked down Mussolini's prison and an airborne expedition was planned by General Student. Skorzeny persuaded Student to allow him to join the striking force with his own party of twenty-six S.S. troops.

The plan was straightforward but required considerable daring and skill. A striking force was to land from gliders on the only stretch of flat ground near the mountain hotel. Another force under Major Mors was to travel by road and seize the funicular station at the foot of the Gran Sasso mountain and so cut the link to the outside world. The striking force took an Italian, General Soleti, with them. He was instructed to order the Italian guards not to open fire.

A group of Mussolini's rescuers on Gran Sasso, September 1943

At two o'clock on 12 September Major Mors and his party waited in their positions round the funicular. They had covered their cross-country route without mishap and waited anxiously for the glider force to appear. Suddenly they heard the drone of the towing planes and with relief they watched the gliders released. Eight gliders landed safely and only one crashed injuring its occupants. Three gliders missed the very difficult landing ground set amidst rocks and boulders on the mountain. General Soleti shot out of the first glider and commanded the Italian guards not to open fire.

There was general confusion as Skorzeny led a group into the hotel to rescue Mussolini. Major Mors, who had come up the funicular, described his meeting with Mussolini:

'In a black overcoat, worn over an old dark blue suit, hat down to his eyes, thus stood the once great man before me. I was shocked. That was Mussolini, the Duce of Italy? I had seen him in his best time, in 1937, when I was with the Italian air force on a friendly visit. Then he was an erect, proud, imposing, personality, full of energy and self-reliance.

'Now he was an old and tired man, used up, visibly ill, with hollow cheeks and unshaved, shaken by the events of recent months. Not sure of himself he stood before these German

The 'old and tired man' rescued by the Germans

soldiers, who greeted him enthusiastically but of whom he only knew that they had come to "liberate" him.'

The bewildered Mussolini was persuaded to board a light aircraft, a Fieseler Storch. This plane had landed on a runway cleared by the paratroops. Skorzeny squeezed into the tiny plane with the pilot and Mussolini. The plane took off and was so overweighted that it nearly crashed on take-off. However, Mussolini was soon transferred to a Heinkel and flown to Vienna. On 13 September Skorzeny spoke on the German radio and told the world that he had liberated Mussolini. Major Mors and his paratroops lodged a formal complaint but were told that Hitler had authorized Skorzeny's speech. Mussolini had become a valuable curio over whom German departments squabbled.

14 Final Moments

The Salo Republic

Hitler was determined that Mussolini should head a renewed Italian Fascist state. The German military leaders were not in favour of such a plan but the Fuehrer was firm. It had become a matter of Fascist prestige that Mussolini should rule again. Mussolini was reunited with his wife, Rachele, and their younger children at Munich. Then on 14 September 1943 he flew north and joined his son Vittorio and his friend Hitler. Mussolini had a number of long talks with Hitler and agreed to set up a new Fascist state in Italy. Hitler urged firm action against the traitors who had betrayed Fascism earlier in the year. Mussolini still wanted time to think and seemed to lack a will of his own. A German observer wrote coldly: 'He is not a revolutionary like the Fuehrer or Stalin.'

On 18 September 1943 Mussolini made a broadcast from Munich and announced that a new Fascist government would be set up in Italy. This announcement plunged Italy into bitter civil war. In the South an Italian government had been formed in the area cleared by the Allies. This government was formed from all parties and partisan groups were formed to fight against the Fascists and the Germans in the north. Longo, a Communist, was one of the ablest partisan leaders. Mussolini's government was formed against the background of the Allied military advance and under the harsh guidance of the Germans.

The Allied advance took time and this gave Mussolini's final government an unnaturally long life. Churchill had spoken of the 'soft underbelly' of the Axis, but to the soldiers fighting their way up Italy there was nothing soft about their task. As Majdalany has written of the ground to be covered: 'No profound tactical knowledge is necessary to appreciate that this country is ideally suited to defence. No sooner has one river or mountain barrier been crossed than another bars the way.'

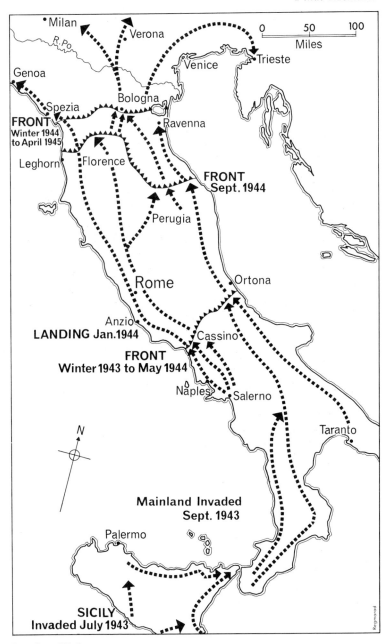

Invasion of Italy 1943–45

Early in 1944 the Allies came up against the Gustav Line hinged on Monte Cassino. A landing was made at Anzio in an effort to draw the Germans from the line. The plan failed and there were four months of terrible fighting before the Allied advance could continue up Route Six. The American 34th division at Cassino 'earned the praise which for soldiers is the best to receive—that of other soldiers who have moved in to relieve them', while the Germans grimly obeyed their orders to hold the line at all costs. Hitler regarded Cassino as another

'Still the Allies pushed on'. Sherman tanks advance while mines explode in the background

battle of the Somme. Still the Allies pushed on and in June 1944 the 5th army entered Rome. In August Florence fell and Alexander was triumphant. Twenty-eight Allied divisions were hard on the heels of twenty-one German divisions. Then the American Chiefs of Staff demanded a landing in the south of France and late in 1944 the weakened Allied advance halted along the German Gothic line from Spezia to Rimini. Mussolini's government was thus allowed to continue into 1945.

Not only did Mussolini have to watch the Allied advance but he also had to listen to German orders. Rahn, the German ambassador, and Wolff, the commander of the S.S. in Italy, haunted Mussolini. Every move that he made was carefully watched as he organized his government. He settled in a villa near Gargnano on the shores of Lake Garda. The government offices were spread out along the lakeside and centred mainly in Salo. The Salo Republic had been formed. Under pressure from the Germans and his own followers Mussolini went ahead

August 1944, Eighth Army troops enter Florence

with plans to punish the Fascists who had deserted him at the moment of crisis. A special tribunal was set up. Its members were Fascists of proved loyalty. Six of those members of the Grand Council who had voted for Grandi's motion had been arrested. Grandi had escaped to Lisbon but Ciano was arrested and placed under an S.S. guard. There could be no doubt as to the verdict which this tribunal would pronounce and Ciano prepared himself for death. His wife, Edda, hoped to trade his life for his diaries and papers, or to persuade her father, Mussolini, to pardon him. A plan was prepared by the Germans. Two picked S.S. men were to stage a rescue so that Ciano could escape in return for his diaries. At the last moment Hitler forbade such a scheme.

The trial took place in January 1944 at Verona. The whole affair was tragic. Most of the members of the Grand Council had acted as they thought best for Italy. Grandi's motion had been tabled and they voted as they saw fit. Marinelli, who was on trial, was deaf and had heard little of the discussion at the Grand Council meeting. Ciano denied conspiracy because the Duce knew of the motion before the meeting. The court sentenced them all to death though poor Marinelli could not even hear the verdict. He fainted when Ciano told him that they were all to die. Mussolini did not intervene though pressed to do so by his daughter.

On 11 January 1944 the prisoners were executed at a shooting range in Verona. A detachment of twenty-five Italian militia carried out the sentence. The prisoners were tied in chairs with their backs to the two rows of the firing squad. The execution was ragged and unpleasant. After the first salvo the prisoners were left groaning and writhing on the ground and the officer in charge had to finish them off with his pistol. In the background stood a German firing squad ready to see that the verdict was in fact carried out.

Mussolini's act of revenge did not strengthen the position of the Salo Republic and it made Mussolini thoroughly miserable. His favourite child, Edda, hated him for allowing her

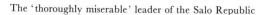

The 'thoroughly miserable' leader of the Salo Republic

husband to die and he became more and more turned in on himself. He even took a morbid interest in all the details of the trial and execution.

The new Fascist government in Italy was now launched, but it lacked any real spirit. The Germans were everywhere and they studied every positive move Mussolini made. He tried to bring in a degree of socialism in the Salo Republic. Businesses of over 100 employees were to be brought under a representative management committee. The Germans regarded such an idea as a betrayal of Fascism while the Italian workers suspected a Fascist trick. There were strikes in Milan and Turin. The Germans acted promptly and 20 per cent of the strikers were deported to labour camps beyond the Alps in Germany. The strikes were broken and Mussolini's experiments in Socialism ended.

Mussolini had to turn to the Germans for help over the formation of an Italian Fascist army. Hitler was not enthusiastic. The Germans preferred to do the fighting themselves and to use the Italians in German labour camps. In the end Hitler agreed that Italian divisions should be trained in Germany to fight within the German military framework. Mussolini's need for armed force was increased by the growing activity of partisans in the North. Graziani, commander of the virtually non-existent army, pointed out that their only hope lay in Hitler's new rocket weapons.

During the summer of 1944 Mussolini made a tour of the four volunteer divisions being trained for him in Germany. He was received with enthusiasm and some of his old fire returned. He began to hope the legions would march again. From this tour of inspection Mussolini went to meet Hitler. On arrival at the station after an unexpected delay Mussolini was greeted by an excited Hitler with the words: 'Duce, an infernal machine has just been let off at me.' Hitler had just survived the bomb plot and he took his friend on a tour of the scene. Then Hitler delivered his usual monologue and stressed the power of his new rockets. Mussolini asked for his Italian divisions and asked that the Italian labour force should be given better treatment in Germany. Hitler's mind was naturally on the bomb plot and for a short time it almost appeared as if Mussolini was a real partner in the Axis alliance. The two dictators parted for the last time and Hitler stressed that he regarded Mussolini as his best if not his only friend.

Upon his return to Italy Mussolini found the situation grim. His government struggled to deal with the growing partisan threat. Fascists were shot in Milan as the partisans learnt that the Allies were just short of Bologna. Mussolini was ill and apathetic. His wife objected to the presence of his mistress, Clara Petacci and he found nothing to take his mind off domestic squabbles. He attempted to make a rousing speech in Milan late in 1944. The attempt was a failure and the end of the Salo Republic was obviously in sight.

Mussolini's Death

On 18 April 1945 Mussolini left Lake Garda for Milan with a German escort. Mussolini was thinking in terms of treating with the Allies. The Germans, who were secretly making their own contacts to arrange peace terms, were determined that he should not make a separate arrangement. The Allied armies in Europe were closing on Berlin and there was not much time left. In Milan Mussolini hoped to be able to approach the Allies through Cardinal Schuster and if needs be he felt that he could escape to the north for a last stand in the Alps.

On 21 April Bologna fell to the Allies and everywhere anti-Fascists hunted down their enemies. Once again the Germans acted before the Italians and Mussolini learnt that General Wolff had arranged the surrender of the German forces in Italy at the very moment that Mussolini himself was talking to Cardinal Schuster about possible terms. On 25 April 1945 Mussolini left Milan and wandered from Como to Menaggio. He was separated from the main body of his Fascist supporters, and the partisans were everywhere. The German forces were streaming back over the Alps, and on the night of 26 April Mussolini and his small party joined a convoy of forty German trucks from an anti-aircraft unit. The convoy was heading for the Tyrol and the men only wanted to reach home peacefully.

On 27 April the column was halted by a rough road block manned by fifteen partisans. The partisans sent for orders from higher authority and, after six hours, the Germans were allowed to go on provided that there were no Italians in their trucks. The trucks moved off leaving Mussolini's party behind. Mussolini had been persuaded to put on a German greatcoat and helmet and to take a place in the back of a truck. The column halted again at Dongo for a final search by the partisans who had been told of Mussolini's presence. He was spotted and hauled from the lorry. The German column went on its way and the Dongo partisans, fiercely proud of their capture, sent to Milan for orders. Clara Petacci managed to join up with Mussolini at this point and they were both housed in a partisan farmer's house.

The Liberation Committee in Milan acted in great confusion. They were afraid that the Allies would take their prisoner and a number of the Communist delegates were determined that Mussolini should die at Italian hands. On the afternoon of 28 April a small group of partisans from Milan called at the farm to collect Mussolini and Clara Petacci. The leader of the group, Valerio, announced that they had come to rescue the Duce. They hurried from the farm to a car and drove down towards the lake. At the Villa Belamonte the car stopped and Mussolini and Clara were bundled out. They were placed against the low wall round the villa and riddled with

'The hatred of the Italian civil war poured out as the Fascist leader was held up for all to see'. The Piazzale Loreto, Milan

bullets at point-blank range. A few moments after the gun-smoke had cleared there was a sudden thunderstorm. The rain splashed down upon the two bodies lying by the roadside.

Fifteen other Fascists were shot by the partisans and their bodies with those of Mussolini and Clara Petacci were taken in a removal van to Milan. There, on the morning of 29 April Mussolini made a final public appearance. His body was hung alongside the body of Clara Petacci and the bodies of four other Fascists from a girder in front of a filling station in the Piazzale Loreto. Fifteen Italians had been shot in this square the previous year by the Germans as a reprisal against partisan activity. Now the hatred of the Italian civil war poured out as the Fascist leader was held up for all to see.

The Allies ordered that the bodies should be moved that evening and Mussolini was buried secretly in a Milan cemetery. Twelve years later his body was moved by his family to the home cemetery at Predappio. A small marble cross marks the spot at which Clara Petacci died for love of Mussolini.

15　Italy since 1945

Government

The Italians in 1945 hoped that their efforts on the side of the Allies would help to cancel out the stain of Fascism. All over Italy people gathered uneasily to discuss the future. Few could continue to hound Fascists as most had accepted Mussolini's rule without serious question. It was better to put thoughts of Fascist rule aside and concentrate on the future. Before the question of the form of Italian government could be decided, a peace settlement had to be made. Italy had to pay reparations to Russia, Yugoslavia, Greece, Albania and Abyssinia. The other powers gave up their claims to such payments. Yugoslavia took over some islands in the Adriatic, and the Dodecanese went to Greece. Trieste was placed under Anglo-American control until 1954 when the city was handed to the Italians and the rest of the area in dispute to Yugoslavia. Italy had to give up all her colonies and dreams of a new Roman empire soon faded. Libya became an independent state in 1951 and ten years later Italian Somaliland gained independence. In 1952 Abyssinia and Eritrea were federated to form an independent empire.

The form that the new Italian government should take became the great topic for discussion. The partisan groups in the North had strong Communist leanings and they gained great influence. They had fought to restore Italian prestige and their opinions were listened to with respect. The question of the position of the monarchy was the prime topic of conversation. The Allies supported the King because they were uncertain as to the reliability of the anti-Fascist groups in the North. A national vote was arranged as to whether or not there should be a King of Italy. Victor Emmanuel had withdrawn from public life when Rome was liberated in 1943. His son, Umberto, was more popular than his father and in 1946 Victor Emmanuel decided to abdicate in favour of his son. In this way he hoped to remove any hint of Fascist connections from the throne. His move proved to be too late. The 'wind from the North' had influenced Italian opinion and the Italian people voted for a republic by a majority of two million votes. A majority of only nine per cent of the valid votes cast. The shield of the House of Savoy was removed from the national flag and Umberto II had to leave Italy after a reign of thirty-four days.

Elections were held and a new government under the Christian Democrat, de Gasperi, was set up. Women voted for the first time in Italy in these elections. The government began the task of drawing up a new constitution. A task that was to take two years to complete. The new constitution came into force on 1 January 1948.

The Italian parliament has two chambers. The senate contains members who are elected on a regional basis while a few members are nominated for life membership by the president. The chamber of deputies contains members elected for five years by universal suffrage. One deputy represents 80,000 electors. The leader of the majority party forms a cabinet and can only be defeated by a vote of censure. The president, or head of state, must be over fifty years of age and is elected for seven years by both chambers acting together. Certain special bodies see that the constitution is carried out. In 1955 the constitutional court was set up to deal with problems raised by laws and decrees.

The new constitution laid down that the Fascist party should not be revived in Italy. In addition it laid down that regional governments should be set up. This was an attempt to destroy Fascist centralization. Italy was divided into ninety-two provinces, each under a prefect, and four special regions, Sicily, Sardinia, Val d'Aosta, Trentino-Alto Adige, under a government commissioner and a local parliament. Plans to extend the regional idea have not yet developed.

In the period immediately following the war the Christian Democrats held sway. In the elections of 1953 they lost their majority over all other parties. The problem of forming coalitions appeared once again in Italian politics. The leaders of the Christian Democrats carried out a series of complicated negotiations to gain support from other parties. A policy of joining with the left developed, the policy of *apertura a sinistra*. After a year of this experiment the elections of 1963 were held and there was cautious encouragement for this policy, though the Communists made gains throughout the country. Moro, the prime minister, gained a vote of confidence from both houses early in 1964 and his government has begun a programme which contains a five-year economic plan along with a pledge of no further nationalization. Electricity had already been nationalized. It remains to be seen whether or not this Catholic-Socialist collaboration can bring stability to Italian politics.

The new constitution confirmed the Concordat with the Roman Catholic Church made in 1929. Mussolini's work in this field remained. Provision for religious teaching in schools was made and divorce was not recognized within the Italian State.

Economic Recovery

The governments within the framework of the new constitution have been given a real chance of stability by the economic advance in Italy since the war. The American loans under the Marshall Plan helped Italian industry in the period immediately after the war. The partisans had saved many industrial plants from destruction and exports of such products as chemicals rose swiftly. Natural gas was discovered in the Po valley and the state-sponsored E.N.I., Ente Nazionale Idrocarburi, developed the source of power. Enrico Mattei, who was killed in an air crash in 1962, led this development and one of the signs of his activity can be seen all over Italy today. Outside many petrol stations hangs the sign of a black, six-footed wildcat on a yellow background. This is the A.G.I.P. petrol sign and A.G.I.P. is a subsidiary company of E.N.I. Three nuclear power plants are also being developed in Italy and the country has risen to eighth place among the world producers of steel. This industrial advance has been encouraged by the fact that Italy was one of the founder members of the Common Market set up under the Treaty of Rome in 1957.

Economic problems still remain. There is the basic problem of an adverse balance of payments and the continuing poverty in the South. In Sicily the Mafia, a deep-rooted association which flouts the law, still survives. The government is trying to tackle such problems and reformers like Danilo Dolci have done much to arouse sympathy and interest in the conditions in the backward areas. Land reform has been attempted and some of the land from badly run big estates has been taken and distributed among the peasants. Advisory centres have been set up to encourage improved farming methods. In 1950 a special Fund for Southern Development was set up and the money used to improve roads, reclaim land and build dams. Ten years later a steel plant was set up in Taranto and works of this sort may bring new wealth to the South. The problem is still present today and many have moved from the South to the wealthier North in their search for employment.

Italian economic life is thriving and, at the same time, Italy has taken her place as one of the countries ready to defend Europe. Since 1950 her army has been reconstructed and is made up of over fifteen divisions of various types. In 1960 Italy placed three air brigades, each of seventy-five aircraft, at the disposal of N.A.T.O.

The Italians have achieved great things since Fascism was

'A sign of the spirit of the Italy built since 1945.' A highway near Bologna

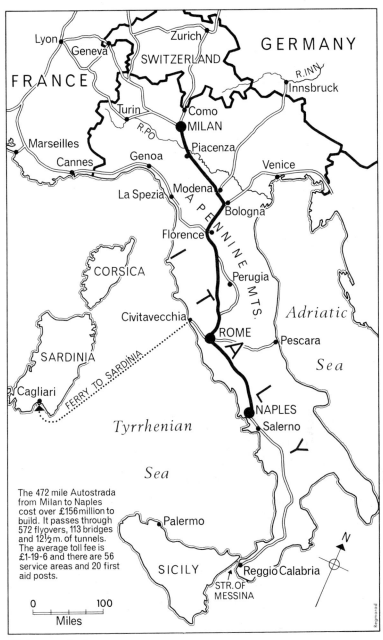

The 472 mile Autostrada from Milan to Naples cost over £156 million to build. It passes through 572 flyovers, 113 bridges and 12½ m. of tunnels. The average toll fee is £1-19-6 and there are 56 service areas and 20 first aid posts.

Highway to the Sun

overthrown. In 1964 the road tunnel beneath the Great Saint Bernard Pass was opened. This feat of engineering was begun in 1958 when tunnels were begun on opposite sides of the pass by Italian and Swiss engineers. In 1962 the tunnels met deep under the Alps. Now the countries are linked by a tunnel over three and a half miles long which is approached by roads protected from the heavy snow by great stone galleries. In the same year the Milan underground railway was opened and the *autostrada del sole*, the Highway of the Sun, linking Milan and Naples was completed. The sweeping motorways linking Italian cities are a sign of the spirit of the Italy built since 1945. An Italy built without the bluster and pomp of Mussolini's time.

Perhaps the finest symbol of the new Italy is the rebuilt abbey of Monte Cassino. The abbey was rededicated by Pope Paul VI in 1964. Twenty years before it had been destroyed in the battle against the Axis. Today it stands renewed. Italians cannot forget Fascism and Mussolini's rule which led to disaster but, since 1945, they have proved that great things can be achieved without the guidance of a dictator.

The rebuilt abbey of Monte Cassino stands out above the military cemetery

During the seventies the basic problems and tensions within
Italy that allowed Mussolini to seize power still showed. In
spite of the wider economic frontiers provided by the European
Economic Community since 1957, and the common farm
policy, the Italian economy has proved weak. There has been
serious unemployment, especially in the South, since the early
sixties. In many parts of Sicily the peasants still burn all the
farmyard manure and life is still very poor in much of the
South of Italy. An awareness of economic weakness and the
ineffectiveness of slogans and 'battles' has not solved the
problem.

The relationship between Church and State has also
developed slowly. There has been a revival of religion under
Pius XII and John XXIII. This has been equalled by a
lively lay cultural movement. Italian films, sculpture, archi-
tecture and fashions are admired throughout the Western
world. Divorce was permitted in Italy in 1970 and the tension
between Church and State remains. Nowhere is this more
clearly to be seen than in the political system. Many fear the
control of the Church and some talk of 'clerical fascism'. In
fact there is more danger from political instability than control.
Between 1946 and 1976 there have been twenty-six governments under twelve prime ministers. Since 1974 the Communists have gained great success in municipal elections and
there has been growing urban violence. In 1976 the Christian
Democrats under Andreotti were able to form a minority
government in the face of the growing Communist challenge.
In 1978 the 'Red Brigade' seized and then murdered Moro,
a respected Christian Democrat leader. Some Italians un-
doubtedly wonder whether the only solution to such political
instability is a dictator.

Mussolini certainly worked hard to build up and leave a
legend that only a dictator could bring Italy to greatness. The
problems facing any Italian government are enormous and
remain: the poor economy, the divisions between North and
South and between rich and poor, the relations between
Church and State, the instability of the political system. In
spite of slogans and conceit Mussolini did not solve the problems. Fascism led to complete disaster and defeat. The
seventies have brought out the fact that there are no simple
solutions for Italy. There are positive growth points but the
development of a modern industrial democratic state is
proving slow and painful.

Further Reading

Books about Mussolini

BENITO MUSSOLINI, *My Autobiography*. Hutchinson, 1939.

RACHELE MUSSOLINI, *My Life with Mussolini*. Hale, 1959.

LAURA FERMI, *Mussolini*. University of Chicago Press, 1961.

CHRISTOPHER HIBBERT, *Mussolini*. Longmans, 1962: Penguin Books, 1965.

ROY MACGREGOR-HASTIE, *Day of the Lion*. Macdonald, 1963.

SIR IVONE KIRKPATRICK, *Mussolini, Study of a Demagogue*. Odhams, 1964.

Works on Special Aspects of Mussolini's Rule

COUNT G. CIANO, *Ciano's Diary*, ed. Malcolm Muggeridge. Heinemann, 1947.

F. W. DEAKIN, *The Brutal Friendship, Mussolini, Hitler and the fall of Italian Fascism*. Weidenfeld & Nicolson, 1962.

DENIS MACK SMITH, 'Mussolini, Artist in Propaganda', *History Today*, April 1959.

Books about Italy

MURIEL GRINDROD, *Italy*. O.U.P. (The Modern World Series), 1964.

DENIS MACK SMITH, *Italy*. University of Michigan Press.

JANET TREVELYAN, *A Short History of the Italian People*. Allen & Unwin, 1959.

General and Fiction

G. GUARESCHI, *The Little World of Don Camillo*. Gollancz.

CARLO LEVI, *Christ stopped at Eboli*. Cassell, 1949.

F. MAJDALANY, *Cassino, Portrait of a Battle*. Longmans, 1957.

RONALD SETH, *Caporetto, the Scapegoat Battle*. Macdonald, 1965.

IGNAZIO SILONE, *Fontamara*. Panther Books, 1965.

Index